FIVE
GREAT
CATHOLIC
IDEAS

FIVE GREAT CATHOLIC IDEAS

EDWARD WM. CLARK

A Crossroad Book
The Crossroad Publishing Company
New York

The Crossroad Publishing Company
370 Lexington Avenue, New York, NY 10017

Printed in the United States of America

Library of Congress Cataloging-in-Publication Data

Clark, E. W. (Edward W.)
    Five great Catholic ideas / E.W. Clark.
      p. cm.
    ISBN 0-8245-1751-2 (pbk.)
    1. Catholic Church – Doctrines. 2. Theology, Doctrinal – Popular
works. I. Title.
BX1754.C48   1998
230′.2 – dc21   98-9515

1 2 3 4 5 6 7 8 9 10   02 01 00 99 98

Contents

Introduction

This book is an exploration of several foundational principles of Catholic doctrine presented on a level accessible to
a broad range of readers. It is rooted in the conviction that
today many people who are neither professional theologians
nor ministerial students share an interest in the work of theology. Unlike catechetics, which is faith seeking expression in
practice and in teaching, this book is an attempt at theologiz-
ing in the Anselmian sense of "faith seeking understanding."
Catholicism is not a collection of unrelated doctrines discovered by revelation and handed down by magisterial teaching.
There are connections among these doctrines like threads in
a tapestry, juxtaposed and woven together to create a total
design that no one segment alone can fully express. How
these doctrines relate to one another colors and alters and
completes the understanding of each one. The work of theology is to discover the connections, sort out the meaning,
and attempt to fill in the empty spaces that the Artist has de-
signed but not yet unveiled. Theologians, however, whether
proposing new theories or expounding old ones, often work
with definitions and terms and language so technical as
to leave the average, well-educated lay reader totally con-
founded and adrift in unfamiliar waters. Accessible theology,
while it may not have a large and enthusiastic readership, is
intended for that segment of the Church that has moved beyond catechetics and seeks an intellectual dialogue with the

doctrines of the Church. As an expression of accessible theology, this book attempts to offer a theological understanding of the fabric of faith for a non-professional but educated readership.

Unfortunately, polemical groups within the Church today are vigorously at work dividing up the fabric of faith, polarizing the people of God, and staking claims to particular doctrines. At the same time, the Catholic Church is engaged in ongoing dialogue with other Christian communities that have long challenged particular doctrines and a Catholic understanding of faith. Both within and outside the Catholic Church, the common ground seems to be receding and individuals are less able to dialogue respectfully about papal authority, the Eucharist, devotionalism, Church governance, family and life issues, priesthood, social and economic justice, and, above all, liturgy. Each group, and there are more than a few, tends to rally around individual doctrines and to present its particular interpretation of those doctrines as the most authentic expression of Catholic belief and practice. As long as individuals continue to argue over particular expressions of Church doctrine, fruitful dialogue and reconciliation are increasingly less likely to take place. The solution is to back up and rediscover a comfortable place where everyone can engage in respectful discussion. The objective is to achieve that oneness of mind and heart that Jesus prayed would be the characteristic sign of his disciples (John 17:20–23). In a real sense, we can't get there from where we are now, defending particular expressions of doctrine while ignoring the foundational beliefs those formulas are meant to express.

Several years ago, on a Christmas eve, I set out to meet my family at our mountain cabin. I carefully checked the map looking for a shorter way that would reduce the travel time, and I was sure I had found it. The map seemed clear enough. After several hours of driving, I finally found myself at the end of the road, within a mile or two of the cabin, but at the bottom of a box canyon. The only way to get where I wanted to be was to turn back, almost an hour's drive, and find a different and more certain route. I think that, doctrinally, this is where we find ourselves in the Church today. We know where we want to be, but perhaps we can't get there from here. We may need to turn back to where the map is very clear and most everyone is in agreement. Then we can discuss together how to get where we all need to be. At heart, we believe the doctrines are right and their formulations, despite the limitations imposed by time and language, are correct, but often we have boxed them in and seem incapable of moving ahead. Even if we find a more secure place on which we can all agree, there will still be plenty to argue about, but at least we will be on common ground and more willing to argue with respect.

The various doctrines of the Church and the formulas of faith that express them are very often the result of lengthy theological and doctrinal development. In their current form they reflect the theological language and expression of the eras in which they were formulated. Today they are more often the subject of debate than of discussion, more often polemicized than investigated. In reality, they are not so much foundational ideas as they are the flowering and development of still more basic truths of Christian faith. Underlying each of them are doctrinal principles and theological ideas that have been consistently present throughout the long history of the Church. It is precisely these underlying principles and ideas of faith that make it possible for us to interpret Christian doctrines correctly by comprehending how the Church, throughout time, has always held to certain basic theological notions. Doctrines like devotion to Mary, transubstantiation, papal infallibility, sacramental penance, and purgatory are all at the end of the road. What are the great ideas that mapped the way for these formal expressions of faith? What are the great ideas (theological *principles* or *notions,* as John Henry Newman termed them) that moved the minds of the Fathers of the Church and inspired their development of the faith? What are the profound ideas from which flow the more developed doctrines of today, ideas that once comprehended can help us to understand, interpret, and organize our beliefs as Catholic Christians?

In this book, I have selected five theological ideas as foundational to Catholic thought and a fuller understanding of Catholic doctrine. They are not the only great ideas in Catholicism, but they touch the very heart of a Catholic understanding of faith. They underlie the doctrines of salvation, grace, sacramentality, revelation, and tradition. These ideas are not exclusively Catholic, but they are often more associated with Catholicism than with other expressions of Christianity. As presented, these ideas are not defined doctrines of the Church, they are not dogmas, but without them our doctrines and our dogmas make little sense. They go to the very heart of Christianity and are to be found at the very origin of Catholic faith. They are the consistent heritage of Christian believers and have been passed from generation to generation in the lived experience of a living Church. If one were to truly understand all of these ideas and firmly hold each one of them in faith, one would discover what it truly means to be a Catholic Christian, a time-traveling and universal believer in God's self-revelation. Even beyond that, these ideas, these theological notions, these principles of faith offer a solid foundation for open dialogue within the Church and between the churches, a dialogue that moves beyond polemics, rancor, and posturing, a dialogue that involves a studied return to the sources of faith and a critical examination of the data of revelation.

Our goal is to know our faith more authentically, to live it more deeply, to communicate it more effectively, and to secure, in the end, the union of all believers and the full realization of the Kingdom of God. In this quest, a fixed preoccupation with particular formulations of doctrine, formulas that may fail the full expression of the doctrine itself, will not bring us there very soon. We won't get there without first going back to the place from which we started. If, however, we are willing to make that journey back to the beginning, to delve beneath the formulations of faith to the bedrock of belief, to study, to explore, to examine, and to "not cease from exploration," then, in the words of T. S. Eliot, "the end of all our exploring will be to arrive where we started and know the place for the first time."[1]

This book is the fruit of many years of teaching, particularly the last eight years at Saint John's Seminary and Saint John's Seminary College, the seminaries of the archdiocese of Los Angeles. For this reason, I dedicate the book to my students, past and future. I would like also to express a note of gratitude to Michael Leach at Crossroad Publishing Company, who has made this book possible, and to Father John Brennan, SMA, and Father Lawrence Herrera, SJ, both of whom read the manuscript during its development and made invaluable suggestions for its improvement. The fact that I did not always accept their suggestions leaves on my shoulders the burden of its deficiencies.

Finally, several notes about the text itself. Each chapter is divided into three parts — theological idea, related doctrines, and implications for an applied theology. The antiquity and significance of each theological idea is supported and elaborated with references from the New Testament and from the Fathers of the Church. A contemporary understanding of these theological notions is most frequently illustrated with citations from the Second Vatican Council. Selected doctrines are then developed in light of their relationship to this theological principle or idea, briefly illustrating how the content and meaning of the doctrine becomes more apparent as the foundational idea is more clearly understood. Finally, prescinding from formal doctrine, several further implications are presented, illustrating the contemporary significance of this theological idea for understanding and living the Christian life.

Writing for the non-professional reader, I have chosen to cite the works of the Church Fathers with titles in English rather than in the original Latin or Greek. In order to clearly identify these references within the body of patristic literature, however, I have chosen, wherever possible, to cite them according to the sections and subsections identified in the *Patrologia Latina* (PL) and *Patrologia Graeca* (PG) series of J. P. Migne. Although these compendia of the works of the Church Fathers have been largely superseded by more critical editions, the Migne series remain the most comprehensive and accessible for identifying individual citations. In the same light, formal Church statements, other than those of the Second Vatican Council, are cited according to the thirty-sixth edition of the *Enchiridion*

Symbolorum, edited by Denzinger and Schönmetzer (DS). The Abbott translation (1966) of the *Documents of Vatican II* has been used throughout. Finally, several different translations of the New Testament have been utilized; in each case I cite the translation that appears most easily understandable.

Chapter 1

"We Are Saved in Community"

"Do you believe that Jesus is your personal savior?" "Are you saved?" Many of us share the experience of being asked these questions, possibly on more than a few occasions, and usually by a total stranger. How do you respond? What do you reply? If you're like most Catholics, you may find yourself reduced to silence. Or you may respond with your own question, "How does anyone know he's saved — or she's saved?" Or you may answer with a barely audible, "Yes, of course," hoping the stranger will just go away. After all, traditional Christianity has taught us to be skeptical about our own salvation. No matter how well we have lived our lives up to now, there is always the possibility of falling away from faith, turning our backs on God, losing our chance at heaven. In his parables Jesus spoke of casting out the invited wedding guest who showed up inappropriately dressed (Matt 22:13) and of turning away the foolish handmaids who forgot to bring oil for their lamps (Matt 25:11). "The invited are many," he said, "the elect are few" (Matt 22:14). Even St. Paul worried that having preached to others, he himself might be rejected (1 Cor 9:27). Still, as Christians, there is a way that we can answer "yes" to both these questions, and do so with total confidence in the truth of our reply. However, we need, first, to understand the meaning behind the questions being asked.

Each of these questions admits to more than a single interpretation, and the interpretation given to the question by the one who asks it may be significantly different from the understanding of the one who replies. The stranger who asks the question usually has this meaning in mind: In your own experience, do you know Jesus on a personal basis? Do you believe that, out of all the myriads of people in the world, and separate from every one of them, Jesus has entered personally and exclusively into your life and chosen you for salvation? Do you wholeheartedly believe that you are saved, even if no one else you personally know is saved, and that no matter what you should do during the whole rest of your life, if you continue to believe in Jesus' promise to you personally, then you are surely saved? Understood in this light, even St. Paul would have been skeptical about his salvation, for while Paul fully believed in Jesus' fidelity to his promise, he was not so certain of his own fidelity to Christ (2 Tim 2:13). There is, however, another way of looking at these questions, one that is far more traditional in Christianity, reaching back beyond the Fathers of the Church to the earliest preaching of the Gospel, and one to which every faithful Christian can most assuredly answer, "Yes."

Among the oldest and most consistent teachings of the Fathers of the Church is the notion that we are saved not alone, but as members of a community. By faith and through baptism God calls us into the community of the Church, and it is here, within the fellowship of the saved, that we find our salvation. It is true that God calls us each by name, that God reaches into our personal histories and, through faith, summons us to salvation in the Church. However, God does not save us independently and separately from others. God does not so individualize salvation that the only thing that should concern me is to know for certain that I am saved, disregarding what happens to anyone else. Moreover, God does not save me on the basis of my confidence in the providence of the Father and in Jesus as my own private savior, but on the basis of the faith of Jesus, which remains present in the community of his followers and which extends to me as a member of that community. Jesus is not my savior, he is our savior, and we are not saved alone, we are saved in community. This notion was the tradition of Christianity for sixteen centuries before the Reform theologians called for a new understanding of Christianity, for a privatizing of faith and an individualizing of the Christian life; and this notion has continued to be the teaching of Catholicism during all the centuries since.[2]

To truly understand the significance of this notion, we must first come to a realization of what redemption and salvation are about. What does our questioner mean by "salvation" when he or she asks us, "Are you saved?" In the context of religious practice, when people speak of salvation they usually have in mind the idea of eternal reward versus eternal punishment, of going to heaven, of release from all the sinfulness and proclivity to evil that exists in their own lives and in the world around them. They want to be saved from eternal damnation, from the unhappiness of sinful living, from the disparate tugging of a divided heart, from the uncertainties of earthly existence, from inner compulsions and external coercions, from physical sickness and emotional pain, in short, from unhappiness. They want to be saved from unhappiness in all of its forms. They want to be happy. Do you believe that Jesus Christ can save you from personal unhappiness and make you happy forever? Do you believe that Jesus is your personal savior? Certainly I do, but is this all that salvation means?

Salvation is more than being "saved from" something, be it unhappiness, sinfulness, or damnation. Much more importantly, salvation is a matter of being "saved for" something. Outside the religious context, when people speak of "saving" they tend to think more in terms of preserving, protecting, and providing than of rescuing, ransoming, or redeeming. People save pictures to remember friends and preserve happy moments from the past. They save money in the bank to provide for their future, to purchase a new car, to take a vacation. In a deeper religious context, salvation is also a matter of being "saved for" something, not just saved from damnation but saved for union with the Father, not just saved from sinfulness but for Christ-like living, not just saved from temporal unhappiness but for eternal fulfillment in the Spirit. We are saved for living the life of the Trinity. We are saved that we might be divinized or sanctified by our common incorporation into Christ. We are saved that the unity of God's creation might be restored and the Kingdom of God might become a reality, "on earth, as it is in heaven." This is what the Fathers of the Church understood by salvation, not only being rescued from certain disaster, but being preserved for divine glory.

Salvation is intimately connected to redemption itself. Salvation is our personal incorporation into the benefits and the experience of being redeemed by Christ. The Fathers of the Church believed and taught that all evil and disorder in the world came about when human sin destroyed the unity of God's plan in creation. Redemption, in their teaching, is the work of restoration, of recovering that lost unity, not only recovering the supernatural unity of human beings with

God, but equally recovering the unity of human beings with each other and with creation. Through his incarnation as a human being, through his death on the cross and his exaltation to the right hand of the Father, Jesus, the eternal Son of God, made both possible and certain the restoration of unity. As Adam's sin initiated the ever increasing disunity of human existence, Jesus' action initiated the ever increasing restoration of unity.[3] Through his redemptive action Christ will eventually restore all that Adam's sin had destroyed. All creation and every human being now stand under the umbrella of redemption. When any human being becomes incorporated into the grace and work of redemption, that person experiences salvation, and with that experience of salvation comes the commission to share in the very work of redemption. Thus, salvation is our personal incorporation into the experience of redemption. Salvation in this sense, however individually received, cannot be a private matter; it is not exclusive. Because the mission that flows from salvation is a common effort, the reality of salvation cannot be a private experience. Restoring this unity is a work in common. Advancing the Kingdom of God is also a work in common. Even our personal sanctification is a work in common.[4]

According to the divine plan, human beings were meant to live in unity with God and with each other. This was intended as more than a moral union of mutual concern, but as a spiritual union by which all human beings would be supernaturally united with God through sharing the same divinized human nature. Original sin introduced separation, individualization, a breaking apart from one another.[5] When we experience salvation, when we enter into the grace of redemption, we are divinized, sanctified, made holy. Our very

unity with God and with one another is restored, and we
are all brought back to the Father in one body, for when
Christ incorporated himself into our humanity, he incorporated us into himself.[6] In the teaching of the Church Fathers,
St. Paul's doctrine on the community of the faithful as the
body of Christ is no mere metaphor, but a statement of reality, "You are all the body of Christ and individually members
of it" (1 Cor 12:27). Our common human personality has
been restored by Christ's assuming it.

Through salvation we have entered into the very glory of
God, but we have not done so individually and alone. Our
salvation takes place in community. "We, though many, are
one body in Christ, and individually members one of another" (Rom 12:5). St. Irenaeus proclaims, "The Glory of
God is man fully alive, but the life of man is the vision of
God."[7] In the end, he is not referring to each person alone,
nor to any individual human being among us. For Irenaeus,
the fully alive human being is the whole divinized body of
Christ, head and members, the sum of all humanity that has
experienced salvation in God's only Son. Thus, even on the
level of our personal sanctification, our experience of salvation is through the community of Christ's body. If, as the
Church Fathers profess, salvation means sharing in the work
of redemption and finding wholeness and holiness in the one
divinized body of Christ, then we are not saved alone; we
are saved in community.

The Church, then, as the body of Christ and the community of his followers, plays an integral and indispensable
role in salvation. A person does not find salvation first and
then decide to join the Church. Rather, it is as a member of the Church that a person finds salvation. Salvation
is experienced through participation in the body of Christ

in a manner that involves both the interiority of faith and the exteriority of presence, both spiritual assent and visible commitment. This notion of salvation in community raises several unavoidable questions about the Church. First, how is the Church involved in the salvation of every person who is saved? Second, how are non-Christians to be saved who are not members of the Church, do not believe in Jesus, and may have never even heard of him?[8]

Before attempting any answer to these two questions, we need to keep in mind the definition of salvation developed above, as well as the testimony of Scripture regarding the universal salvific will of God. Our definition of salvation is essentially communal. It involves not simply our individual rescue from eternal damnation, but our common union with God, with others, and with all creation in the one body of Christ. Moreover, salvation commissions those who are saved to engage in the collaborative task of advancing the Kingdom of God. An essential question of salvation, then, is how does a person become a member of Christ's body, which is essential for salvation, if he or she is not committed to membership in the community of his followers?

At the same time we must not forget that God does not create human beings for damnation. In his first letter to Timothy, St. Paul expresses the constant Christian belief that God "desires all men to be saved and to come to the knowledge of the truth" (1 Tim 2:4). God's "desire" is not simply "wishful thinking." It is an expression of God's will, and God's will is always effective. From what we know of God, we feel certain that God's mind does not conceive any idea that cannot or will not come to exist.[9] If God desires something, God must will it to be. If God so wills the salvation of every person, yet salvation involves fellowship in the com-

munity of Christ, how are they saved who are not members
of the Church? If there is no other name given to humankind
by which we are to be saved except that of Jesus Christ of
Nazareth (Acts 4:12), how, then, are we to understand the
salvation of those who do not know him, those who do not
believe in him, and even those who have purposely rejected
him? Answers might be more easily conceived if salvation
were simply a matter of individual election and personal
commitment. It would be enough, then, simply to acknowledge "those whose faith is known to God alone," without
the need to pray for them as well, for surely they would be
saved without the intervention or prayer of the Church.[10]
However, salvation is not individual and personal, and the
Church does effectively intercede for the salvation of people.
We are saved not alone, but in community.

How then is the Church involved in the salvation of all
who are saved? This question has become one of the pressing issues in contemporary theology.[11] The Fathers of the
Second Vatican Council proclaimed the Church to be the
"universal sacrament of salvation." The Dogmatic Constitution on the Church reflects the understanding of salvation as
the union of human beings with God and with one another
in the community of Christ's body, here identified with the
Church itself. Through the Church, Christ continues to be
active in the world.

> Christ, having been lifted up from the earth, is draw-
> ing all men to himself. Rising from the dead, he sent
> his life-giving Spirit upon his disciples and through this
> Spirit has established his body, the Church, as the uni-
> versal sacrament of salvation. Sitting at the right hand
> of the Father, he is continually active in the world, lead-

ing men to the Church, and through her joining them more closely to himself and making them partakers of his glorious life by nourishing them with his own body and blood.[12]

The Pastoral Constitution on the Church in the Modern World further sees the Church as the instrument of salvific grace, described as "the mystery of God's love for man" by which the salvation of the whole human race will be achieved.

> While helping the world and receiving many benefits from it, the Church has a single intention: that God's kingdom may come, and that the salvation of the whole human race may come to pass. For every benefit which the people of God during its earthly pilgrimage can offer to the human family stems from the fact that the Church is "the universal sacrament of salvation," simultaneously manifesting and exercising the mystery of God's love for man.[13]

The role of the Church in universal salvation and the restoration of creation itself is asserted in the Decree on the Missionary Activity of the Church.

> The Church has been divinely sent to all nations that she might be "the universal sacrament of salvation...." As the salt of the earth and light of the world, the Church is summoned with special urgency to save and renew every creature. In this way all things can be restored in Christ, and in him mankind can compose one family and one people.[14]

Finally, the Dogmatic Constitution on the Church clearly asserts that the Church is the instrument of Christ for the salvation of all who are saved. "Established by Christ as a fellowship of life, charity, and truth, it is also used by him as an instrument for the redemption of all, and is sent forth into the whole world as the light of the world and the salt of the earth" (*Lumen Gentium,* 9). Salvation, described as the union of human beings with God, with one another, and with all creation in the community of Christ's fellowship, continues to be effected in the world by Christ acting through the instrumentality of the Church.

It was due to the redemptive sacrifice of Christ, which Scripture describes as a priestly act that shall never pass away (Heb 7:24–25), that the economy of salvation was reestablished in the world. Scripture proclaims that this economy was God's divine plan in creation, hidden for ages and generations but now made manifest in the Church (Eph 3:9; Col 1:26). It is through the continual celebration of that sacrifice that salvific grace continues to be present and operative in the world.[15] It is inconceivable that God would have established multiple economies for the salvation of humankind. Indeed, as we have seen, "There is salvation in no one else, for there is no other name under heaven given among men by which we must be saved" (Acts 4:12).

Thus, by design, the salvific grace that flows from the redemptive activity of Christ continues to be present in the world, reuniting all creation with the Father. By design, the Holy Spirit continues to make that grace available to everyone who is saved. By design, that grace continues to be present and operative in the world because the Church is present and operative in the world. In the one divine economy, wherever and for whomever the grace of Christ is effective, grace and the full means of salvation are available only through the presence and mediation of the Church.[16] If there is no salvation outside of Christ, then the Church is necessarily involved in the salvation of every person who is saved. In a real sense, without the Church there is no salvation; but what of those who are outside the Church? How are they to be saved? Specifically, how is the non-Christian and the non-believer to be saved through the instrumentality and mediation of the Church?

God desires the salvation of all people; we know that to be an established fact of revelation. We also believe in the necessary effectiveness of God's universal salvific will. However, there are millions of people in the world who are not Christians. It is probable that the majority of them have never heard of Jesus Christ. In the centuries since Jesus ascended to the Father, there were millions more who never came to know Jesus or profess faith in him. However, if salvation involves fellowship in the community of Christ, how are they saved who do not know Jesus and are not members of his Church? How are non-Christians to be saved who do not believe in Jesus and may never have heard of him? We have just seen that without the Church there is no salvation, but is salvation still possible for those who are outside the Church? This is a question that the Church has returned to again and again throughout its history.

In the early Church and throughout the patristic period the common belief was that God would save the "just person" through the grace of Christ present in the world, even if he or she did not know Christ.[17] Of particular note is St. Augustine's teaching on the implicit knowledge of Christ. From the beginning of the human race, all those who lived a good and devout life, implicitly following the commands of Christ whenever and wherever they lived, undoubtedly were saved by him.[18] In effect, they were members of the Church even before the Church came to be.[19] Moreover, the grace of salvation would be made available to those who, through no fault of their own, did not know or believe in Jesus. Nonetheless, the possibility of truly being a "just person" without knowing Christ and becoming a member of his body was considered to be very slim indeed; and certainly, without becoming a member of the Church, one could not participate fully in the grace and mission of salvation nor, through prayer, call upon the true source of salvation.

Familiar to this argument was the passage from St. Paul, "But how are men to call upon him in whom they have not believed? And how are they to believe in him of whom they have never heard? And how are they to hear without a preacher? And how can men preach unless they are sent?" (Rom 10:14). On the other hand, for those who came to know and believe in Jesus but refused membership in the Church, the grace of salvation was likewise rejected. More specifically, those who abandoned the Church through heresy, apostasy, or schism also abandoned the grace of salvation. For them, having once been in the Church, to now be outside the Church was to be outside the sure knowledge of salvation itself. Speaking to those who had rejected the Church in which they once believed, Origen stated, "Let no one persuade himself, let no one deceive himself: outside this house, the church, no one is saved. For if anyone goes outside, he is responsible for his own death."[20] Certainly for the Fathers of the Church, salvation was a matter of living the just life within the community of the Church, for only there was salvation assured.[21]

In time the leadership of the Church, as well as the faithful, came to believe that the Gospel had, in fact, been preached to all nations, and that, with few exceptions, the

only ones now outside the Church were those who had rejected the Gospel and fellowship in the community. Thus, in
the fifteenth century the maxim "Outside the Church there
is no salvation" was hurled at the followers of Orthodoxy
who remained in schism from the Roman Church.[22] The
picture totally changed a century later with the discovery
of the new world. Suddenly there appeared untold numbers of people who, through no fault of their own, had
not heard the Gospel or believed in Jesus and his Church.
The Church's theologians, however, now went beyond simply retrieving the former belief in the salvation of those who
were implicitly members of the Church through their implicit
faith in Christ.[23] Some now proclaimed that even those to
whom the Gospel had been preached still might not be cul-
pable for their lack of faith in Christ and membership in the
Church if the Gospel had not been preached to them in a
convincing manner. Culpability might be placed on the defective preaching and modeling of the Gospel rather than on
the stubbornness and perfidy of the hearer.[24] In the twen-
tieth century, Father Leonard Feeney of Boston interpreted
the dictum "Outside the Church there is no salvation" in
the most restrictive manner when he proclaimed that no one
could be saved who was not a member of the Roman Catholic Church. Because of his refusal to recant this position, he,
himself, was formally excommunicated with the approval of
Pope Pius XII in 1949.[25]

All of this stands as prologue for the teaching of the Second Vatican Council. In the Dogmatic Constitution on the
Church, the Council Fathers clearly taught that those who
are without formal membership in the Church, in particular those who have not yet received the Gospel, may still
be saved because they are "related in various ways to the

People of God" (*Lumen Gentium,* 16). Because of this relationship to God's People, varied though it may be, their reception of salvation remains both through and in community. Divine providence does not deny the help necessary for salvation even to those "who, without blame on their part, have not yet arrived at an explicit knowledge of God, but who strive to live a good life, thanks to his grace" (*Lumen Gentium,* 16). Nonetheless, whosoever, "knowing that the Catholic Church was made necessary by God through Jesus Christ, would refuse to enter or to remain in her could not be saved" (*Lumen Gentium,* 14). Thus, while it is always true to say, "*without* the Church there is no salvation," it is not equally true to say, "*outside* the Church there is no salvation."

The Church is involved in the salvation of every person who is saved. Even the non-Christian finds salvation through an implicit relationship to the people of God, the Church, for it is through the Church that the grace of salvation continues to be present and operative in the world. No one can enter the Kingdom of God alone, for the Kingdom of God is made visible and real in the community of God's People; and no one can advance the Kingdom of God alone, but only in collaboration with all who have been commissioned in salvation. For those who truly understand the nature of salvation, belonging to the Church is not an option. One does not find salvation and then elect to enter the Church. Rather, through membership in the community of the saved, one uncovers salvation. One is led by grace to join the Church, and within the Church one finds salvation. Nonetheless, joining the Church, in itself, is not enough. "He is not saved, however, who, though he is part of the body of the Church, does not persevere in charity. He remains indeed in the bosom of the Church, but, as it were, only in a 'bodily' manner and not 'in his heart'" (*Lumen Gentium,* 14). On the other hand, if one remains faithful to the Church, both in faith and in action, then one can be assured of salvation and proclaim with total confidence, "Yes, I know that I am saved."

It was with this confidence, near the end of his life while languishing in prison and awaiting death, that St. Paul wrote to his disciple Timothy, "I have fought the good fight, I have finished the race, I have kept the faith. From now on a merited crown awaits me; on that Day, the Lord, just judge that he is, will award it to me — and not only to me, but to all who have looked for his appearing with eager longing" (2 Tim 4:7–8). Faithful to the Church to the end, faithful to the whole community that together awaited the return of the Lord with eager longing, St. Paul was at last confident about his salvation, because he was certain that we are not saved alone, but in community.

Jesus is *our* savior, not *my* savior. Yes, he is personal to me, but he is not exclusive to me, and he does not save me separately from others. In fact, he saves me by making me part of his body, part of his Church. How well this is expressed in our frequent recitation of the Lord's Prayer. We pray to *our* Father in heaven, not to *my* Father. The whole context of the prayer is the community of faith — give *us* this day our daily bread, forgive *us* our trespasses, deliver *us* from evil. Even when we recite this prayer alone in the silence of our hearts or in the privacy of our rooms, we are conscious of praying together with the whole community of God's people. There is simply no other way to say "Our Father" than in conscious association with our fellow citizens in the Kingdom of God. We pray with the solicitude of brothers and sisters who know in the innermost recesses of our hearts that we are not alone, that what affects any one of us affects all of us, most of all salvation itself. "If one member suffers, all the members suffer with it; if one member is honored, all the members share its joy. You, then, are the body of Christ. Every one of you is a member of it" (1 Cor 12:26–27). I am aware that Jesus personally calls me into the community of faith and salvation. Therefore, as long as I understand salvation as inclusive of others and not exclusive to myself, I can truthfully refer to Jesus as my "personal savior."

There is yet another dimension to Jesus as "our personal savior," whether we are Christian or not, whether we know him personally or not. Jesus himself remains a person, even now in glory. The risen Christ cannot be separated from the Jesus of history and reduced to a universal principle, an abstract idea, or an expression of "God-consciousness" through which salvation becomes attainable. This is true despite the efforts of nineteenth-century rationalists or even twentieth-century members of the Jesus Seminar to divide the identity of Jesus Christ.[26] Through particular historical events, Jesus showed himself to be the fullness of revelation and the mediator of salvation. Even now, liberated from the very bonds of time and space that defined his earthly existence, Jesus continues to mediate salvation from the center of his personal existence. It is not the "idea of Christ" but the very person of Jesus, fully divine and fully human, who calls us to salvation within his Church and through the community of the Church makes salvation possible. Even though we claim Jesus as our personal savior, however, it does not alter the truth of revelation that we are each called to salvation, not alone, but in community.

Related Doctrines

It is apparent, then, that important doctrines of the Church follow necessarily from this fundamental notion of salvation in community. Among these doctrines, as we have already seen, are the necessity of salvation in Christ and the person of Jesus as the universal Savior of humankind. No one is saved except through Jesus. Multiple economies of salvation do not exist, such that some should be saved explicitly by Jesus while others are saved implicitly by the Spirit of God. Rather, if we proclaim, with St. Basil, that wherever the action of the Holy Spirit is found, there also is found the action of the Son of God,[27] then it remains impossible to exclude the saving activity of Christ from the saving activity of the Holy Spirit. Even to speak of the salvific mediation of non-Christian religions is not to exclude the necessary efficacy of Christ's saving action nor the necessary instrumentality of the Christian community.

The Church

The very nature and necessity of the Church likewise follows from this theological notion of salvation in community. The Church is not a free association of individuals who have come to know Christ personally and to believe in his salvific role in human history. Nor is the Church simply a community of Christians who support one another in living their faith, band together in the performance of charitable works in Jesus' name, find solace and encouragement in communal worship, and preach the Gospel worldwide with the intent of saving countless individuals from the fires of eternal damnation. The Church does not exist to be a support group for the individual Christian, although it has often been reduced to that role in the experience of those adherents who feel compelled to come and go, as personal circumstances dictate.

Rather, the Church is the body of Christ made visible, whose members are inseparable from one another, the advance agent of the Kingdom of God, continuing to increase in every dimension until the whole of creation is encompassed, and the community of salvation whose very presence in the world makes possible the salvation of every human being and without whose presence salvation is not accessible. The Church is the sacrament of Christ, continuing to mediate the fullness of revelation and salvation through historical occurrences and events, as Jesus himself did. The Church is the sole means established by Christ for the full restoration of the divine plan in creation and the final reconciliation of humankind with God. Although structured as an institution, the Church is, above all, the people of God. Those who truly understand the nature of the Church become committed to its mission and know that salvation for them is not possible outside its ranks.

Infant Baptism

Likewise, the doctrine of infant baptism, inexplicable in terms of the sacrament as an expression of personal faith commitment, rests solely on this theological principle of salvation in community.[28] Until the fourth century, the primary purpose for baptism was inclusion in the faith community and membership in the body of Christ. Certainly, membership in Christ assured the forgiveness of sin, but the notion of release from original sin had yet to be raised, let alone dominate the discussion of Christian baptism. Almost universally, the Church, both East and West, encouraged the baptism of infants and children whose parents converted to the Christian faith as an assurance that the children themselves would be included in salvation.[29] Even children born of two Christian parents most often were baptized as a sign of membership in the saving community. It was more frequent to delay the baptism of a child born of parents who were not both Christian, especially if the non-Christian parent objected, or of children who were older when their parents converted and who were approaching the age of personal decision themselves. In cases of emergency, however, where life was threatened, even these children were baptized.

In every instance where infant baptism took place, and there is no doubt that it was the general practice throughout the Church, it was in response to the faith of the parents and of the Christian community. The universal belief was that incorporation in the community of faith assures salvation. For those who had not yet arrived at personal faith commitment, nothing more than membership in the faith community was required. For those who had already arrived at faith, only willful separation from the community could result in the loss of salvation, and refusal to accept baptism in itself constituted willful rejection of the community. An older child or adult who came late to faith in Christ and sought membership in the Church was fully aware that it was baptism into the Christian community that assured salvation, not an independent commitment to Christ devoid of any attachment to the Church itself. From the earliest days of Christianity, the doctrine of infant baptism bears testimony to the notion of salvation in community and finds its justification in this theological principle.

Implications for an Applied Theology

From this early Christian notion that we are saved not alone
but in community, many potential implications arise for
understanding faith and living the Christian life. Four such
implications involve the purpose of the sacraments, the intent of liturgy, the nature of Christian moral teaching, and
the Christian experience of death.

The Purpose of the Sacraments

Often the tendency is to think of the sacraments as moments
of personal encounter with God or as private experiences of
a life lived within the Church. We turn the focus inward and
see ourselves, individually, as the primary recipients of each
sacrament. The reality is, however, that the sacraments are
not intended for us, individually, but for us as a community. The primary recipient of each sacrament and of every
sacramental enactment is the Church itself. Through the Eucharist, the whole Church is nourished as the body of Christ.
Through sacramental penance, the whole Church is con-
firmed in the grace of repentance and made the instrument
of reconciliation in the world. Through baptism, the entire
Church is enlarged and strengthened as the community of
salvation, just as Confirmation renews the commission of the
Church in evangelization and service. Through the Anointing
of the Sick, the faith of the entire community is strengthened
to face the crisis, dissolution, and momentary despair with
which nothing in life so consistently confronts us as does
serious illness, lengthy infirmity, old age, and, ultimately,
death. In holy orders, the entire Church is continually re-
focused as the priestly, prophetic, and kingly people of God,

sharing together in the universal priesthood of Christ and, together, exercising spiritual stewardship over creation; as the ordained priest is *Alter Christus* for the Church, so the whole Church, as the body of Christ, is *Alter Christus* for the world. Finally, in sacramental marriage, the covenant between Christ and his Church is renewed in and through the blessed commitment of his disciples, who are still sent forth two by two to spread the good news of the Reign of God in our lives and in our homes.

Because we, as individuals, receive the sacraments with a focus on ourselves and on our own spiritual growth, we tend to think of the sacraments in private and personal terms. In reality, with each sacramental encounter we receive the grace of that sacrament because we are members of the Church. We participate in the grace of the sacraments we receive, but that grace is never reserved for us alone. Through our sharing in the sacraments, the Church itself grows in grace. As individuals, we are the conduits of grace, the mediators of grace for the entire community of faith. As individuals, we may personally encounter God in numerous and diverse ways — in the silence of prayer, during a quiet walk in the mountains or while gazing in stillness at the majesty of an ocean sunset, in pondering the words of Scripture, in the encounter of human intimacy, or in compassionate service to one in need. Our personal encounters with God could never be restricted to the sacraments; but the sacraments, together with the proclamation of Scripture, are the primary means for the whole community of the Church to come into intimate contact with God. Just as we are saved not alone but in community, so also we receive the sacraments not as individuals but as members of the Church. The primary recipient of each sacrament is the Church.

The Intent of the Liturgy

Sacraments are liturgical expressions, and what is true of sacraments individually is true of liturgy as a whole. Liturgy, the highest expression of which is the celebration of the Mass,[30] is not private prayer but public worship. Liturgy is what the Church does together in praising God and making accessible the grace of Christ in the world. There are few aspects of the Church so capable of surfacing division or creating controversy among the faithful as is liturgy. People at all points on the theological spectrum hold to liturgy like a private possession and become disturbed by any deviation from their own spiritual or aesthetic preferences. In the reform of the liturgy, the Fathers of the Second Vatican Council called for a renewed appreciation of the communal nature of liturgical celebration and established fuller expression of the public and communal nature of worship as one of the guiding principles for the reform of the rites.[31] While it is important to celebrate liturgy in a manner that is sensitive to the spiritual expression of the immediate congregation, the public and communal nature of liturgical worship must never be underplayed or sacrificed. Private prayer should be adapted to the spiritual preferences of the individual, but liturgy, which is not private prayer, expresses the entire community of salvation gathered in worship.

The Nature of Christian Moral Teaching

Perhaps the most encompassing implication derived from the notion of salvation in community affects the Christian understanding of morality. In contemporary society, personal freedom, individualism, and privacy are often touted as the hallmarks of moral decision-making and behavior. If no one else gets hurts, an action is often considered morally justified. If all the parties involved consent to an action, most often their decision is upheld as the standard of moral behavior, unless it is a clear violation of statutory law. Even when the letter of the law is broken, individuals will claim to have done nothing morally wrong. What is morally offensive to one person, may not be so considered by another. When salvation itself is so often viewed as a matter of personal conscience and private experience, it is not difficult to envision moral standards constructed on the same norms of individual freedom and personal determination. However, a different standard comes into play when salvation is understood as a communal experience and responsibility. Now the collective wisdom of a graced community determines the norms of moral behavior, a community with a collective history, a collective social conscience, and a collective commitment to the future. Even hidden, private actions are understood to have a social dimension and a communal effect when the very notion of salvation is understood as communal and not private.

The Christian Experience of Death

Most religious people have always understood their present moral behavior to affect their future destiny. Whether that future be an eternal afterlife as Christians conceive it, be understood as the endless process of regeneration endorsed by several of the world's great religions, or follow any number of possible configurations reflective of religious belief, most religious systems have taught that what we do in this life determines what happens to us in the next. As Chris-

tians, we pray that we may always "live in this passing world
with our hearts set on the world that will never end."[32] The
great fear, of course, is that we will not consistently live our
lives with the focus of commitment and the purity of intention worthy of such a heaven. When to this fear is added a
concept of salvation as a private and individual experience
ratified in isolated judgment before God, what results is an
image of death that is fearful and isolated, the dissolution of
relationships and the loss of personal attachments. In death,
it is said, we stand alone before God and have nothing to
testify on our behalf except our personal faith in Jesus and,
possibly, the good deeds reflective of that faith. On the other
hand, we have all the evil deeds of our lives to accuse us.

How un-Christian, in fact, this image is! In reality, if we
have found salvation within the community of Christ's followers, if we have lived our lives within that community of
faith and, despite our occasional lapses and sins, have always
turned back in fidelity to that community, then we do not die
alone and we do not stand alone in judgment before God.
Rather, we are accompanied by all those who went before
us "marked with the sign of faith," a fact to which we testify each time we recite the first Eucharistic Prayer at Mass.
At death, millions of fellow Christians will welcome us into
heaven and stand with us before God, proclaiming, "This
one, too, is a Christian." As long as we remain faithful to
the Church, the community of salvation, we can be certain of
our salvation in Christ. The ultimate testimony that we are
saved not alone, but in community, is that even in death we
do not stand alone. We have fellowship in the communion
of saints.

Chapter 2

"The Kingdom of Heaven Begins on Earth"

We live in an age of sometimes amazing contradictions. When we examine closely the profile of the American people, we are struck by the complexity of current attitudes and opinions. As a people, we become upset with individuals who fail to conform to our own cherished ways of thinking, yet we claim great value for personal freedom. We applaud entertainers, athletes, politicians, and other public figures even when they defy the common standards of moral behavior, yet we profess the importance of personal integrity. We pride ourselves on the realism and practicality of our thinking, yet are mesmerized by thoughts of extraterrestrial visitors and new age religions. We discount an afterlife of reward or punishment, yet demonstrate increasing fascination with ideas of reincarnation and the transmigration of souls. We disclaim any real belief in the supernatural on the level of faith and religion, yet are unduly attracted to tabloid stories of the supposed supernatural in everyday life. We dismiss notions of spiritual power explained by divine origination, then expect science to resupply those same powers based on natural causality.

Those who believe in the traditional tenets of religious faith are often discounted, marginalized, or dismissed, yet those who offer freshly fabricated notions of pseudo-religious content, frequently outrageous in nature, attract large followings. The "true believer" is no longer the person who demonstrates conviction in an established religion, but the individual who is totally committed to an ideology or a cause. The root of these amazing contradictions is an exterior projection of no-nonsense practicality and an interior desire for transcendence and the supernatural. The good news is that the supernatural does, in fact, exist and is part of our everyday lives, that transcendence is the human condition, and that there is more to reality than the human eye can perceive. This, of course, has great implications for what it means to be human and for how we live our lives here and now.

Since the earliest days of Christianity, the Church has taught that we live not only a natural life in this world but a supernatural life as well — right here and right now. Deeply rooted in the theology of the New Testament, this notion was the particular development of the patristic period and of medieval scholasticism. The supernatural life is not reserved for heaven; it begins on earth and involves a transformation of the human person, a transformation effected by the indwelling of the Holy Spirit, a transformation elicited by grace. Around this basic conviction, numerous theological notions have been developed. Were the first human beings created in a supernatural state which was then lost by human sin, or were they created with a disposition toward the supernatural life which they never achieved because human sin intervened? Through his death and resurrection (or through the incarnation), did Jesus restore the supernatural state that had been lost, or did he introduce human beings into the supernatural life they had never before known? Regardless of which positions one were to assume, the fundamental revelation remains the same: human beings were created to live the supernatural life, a condition now made accessible to us only through the human existence of the Son of God, Jesus Christ.

While the witness of New Testament Scripture does not refer explicitly to supernatural life or sanctifying grace, terms coined in the patristic and scholastic periods respectively, the New Testament gives ample witness to the transformation of the human person under the influence of Jesus and the Holy Spirit. Numerous passages proclaim the new life that we come to live in Christ through baptism and the Spirit. In the Gospel of John, Jesus informs Nicodemus that "no one can see the reign of God unless he is begotten from above . . . without being begotten of water and Spirit. Flesh begets flesh, Spirit begets spirit" (John 3:3, 5 and 6). Within the context of the Gospel of John, this passage makes clear reference to the effects of baptism and the action of the Holy Spirit. Equally clear in this passage is reference to a fundamental transformation of the human person, already composed of flesh and spirit as is evident from natural birth, but now reborn in spirit through the "supernatural" action of the Holy Spirit. What this passage makes no attempt to clarify is the precondition of the human spirit prior to the regenerative action of the Spirit of God.

In his basic teaching on the effects of law and redemption, St. Paul builds on this notion of human life reborn in Christ. Writing to the Galatians, Paul proclaims that the law can do no more than convict us of sin. Legal observance cannot win salvation. In fact, all attempts to observe the law can only convince us about the impossibility of keeping the law perfectly. Through faith, however, Christ not only saves us but also relieves us of the penalty involved in keeping the law imperfectly. Through his death, Christ not only fulfilled the law but abolished its power over us. By identifying with Christ in his death and resurrection, we find salvation in our attachment to him and not in our futile attempts to keep the law unfailingly. Thus Paul says, "It was through the law that I died to the law, to live for God. I have been crucified with Christ, and the life I live now is not my own; Christ is living in me. I still live my human life, but it is a life of faith in the Son of God, who loved me and gave himself for me" (Gal 2:19–20).

In referring to Christ living in him, Paul is not speaking an analogy about the nature of faith, as if to say that living in the faith of Christ is *like* living the very life of Christ. No. What Paul is proclaiming is his deep conviction that through the indwelling of faith, or of the Holy Spirit who is the source of faith, his natural life has been transformed, although not lost. "I still live my human life," he says, but it is a life fundamentally and essentially changed. It is no longer Paul, the natural man, who lives; it is Christ who lives in Paul, now supernaturally reborn. To argue his point that the law no longer binds us to strict observance under penalty of divine judgment, Paul draws on his conviction about the supernatural transformation of the human person through the indwelling of the Holy Spirit.[33] We who live now on the level of the Spirit will be judged not by our natural attachment to the law but by our supernatural attachment to Christ. Such attachment would be impossible without the indwelling of the Holy Spirit and the supernatural transformation of the human person.

One final passage of Scripture must not be overlooked. It serves to focus our attention on the truth that this new life in Christ, this supernatural state of being, is not something delayed for the future or realized only after death. Rather, it begins now, here, in this life. St. Paul appeals to the Christians at Rome to set aside all attachment to sin and to recognize the call to live their lives in Christ right now. He writes:

> Are you not aware that we who were baptized into Christ Jesus were baptized into his death? Through baptism into his death we were buried with him, so that, just as Christ was raised from the dead by the glory of the Father, we too might live a new life. If we have been united with him through likeness to his death, so shall we be through a like resurrection. This we know; our old self was crucified with him so that the sinful body might be destroyed and we might be slaves to sin no longer. (Rom 6:3–6)

Paul is not speaking of a supernatural transformation that will be realized only in the future. The old self has already died through baptism; the new self has already risen in Christ. Even the body shall experience in the future the resurrection that the human person has already experienced in baptism. Paul concludes, Jesus' death "was death to sin, once for all; his life is life for God. In the same way, you must consider yourselves dead to sin but alive for God in Christ Jesus" (Rom 6:10–11). Changed, transformed, reborn, the baptized Christian already lives the supernatural life of heaven.

This notion, that even here on earth we live the supernatural life, found explicit expression among the Fathers of the Church. Where they disagreed among themselves was over the issue of whether Adam and Eve, as the first human beings, initially possessed the supernatural state and then lost it because of sin, or whether, due to their sin, they never came into possession of that supernatural state which God had intended for them from the beginning. St. Athanasius and St. Gregory of Nyssa, for example, held to the first view,[34] while St. Clement of Alexandria and Origen held to the second.[35] Either what was lost in Adam has been restored in Christ, or, through Christ, humanity has been recreated and elevated to a supernatural condition that Adam never enjoyed. From either perspective, there is definite consensus that after Adam no human being enjoyed the supernatural condition until Christ restored or elevated human beings to the supernatural order.

The Fathers of the Church explicated their doctrine on the basis of Genesis 1:26 and 27. In the first verse, God is said to have created human beings in God's own image and likeness, while the second verse refers only to humanity's creation in the image of God. Beginning with St. Irenaeus at the end of the second century,[36] the Fathers of the Church were nearly unanimous in their teaching that we are all created in the *image* of God, by which they meant that we are endowed with reason and free will, but that we are also recreated in the *likeness* of God through the saving action of Jesus Christ. That *likeness* is variously referred to as "divinization" or as "sanctification." It refers, without doubt, to the supernatural condition. Did God intend to create human beings in both God's own image and likeness but reserved the divine likeness as a pledge of future glory, or did God, in fact, create human beings in both God's image and likeness, such that when the first humans sinned, the divine likeness was lost for all future generations until it was restored in Christ? That question has remained a topic of theological debate throughout the history of Christianity, even to our own day.[37] It is the question of "original justice" and has profound implications for the construction of an authentic Christian anthropology. Nonetheless, there is no uncertainty among the Church Fathers that those who live in Christ have a share in his divine nature and live, even in this world, the supernatural life.

This doctrine of the supernatural life was further elaborated by St. Augustine in his dispute with the followers of Pelagius, who taught that human beings were not dependent on infused grace in order to achieve salvation. Rather, Pelagius maintained that by making proper use of free will anyone is capable of living sinlessly, of following the moral example and teaching of Jesus, and of gaining entrance into the fullness of salvation made accessible through Jesus' redemptive death. Pelagius rejected the notion that following upon the sin of Adam the human will is intrinsically impaired and prone to evil. Rather, human beings fall into sin by personally imitating and reenacting Adam's transgression. Baptism, he maintained, serves to introduce believers into the community of the Church while remitting individual sins and strengthening the will that personal sin has weakened. In Pelagius's writings there is no notion of elevating grace or of human beings entering into the supernatural order. Grace is limited to all forms of divine assistance by which God motivates the individual to make proper use of the human will. His concept of grace excludes the notion of divine indwelling and supernatural elevation. For Pelagius, each person is ordered to salvation, not by grace, but by nature.

In contrast to Pelagianism, St. Augustine taught that human beings are incapable of entering into salvation unless created human nature is somehow elevated to the supernatural state. In his theology, he maintained that Adam was not only created on a natural level, but also endowed with certain preternatural gifts and elevated to the supernatural order. Building upon the Pauline teaching concerning the sin of Adam, that "through one man's disobedience all became sinners" (Rom 5:19), Augustine further developed the doctrine of original sin. When Adam sinned, the supernatural endowment was lost, the preternatural gifts of freedom from unrestrained concupiscence, bodily immortality, and physical impassibility were also lost, and the human will, while remaining intact, became debilitated. Through the act of physical generation, every human being is conceived and born with Adam's sinful inheritance and burdened with the "cruel necessity of sinning."[38]

Only through Christ can the human being be delivered from the state of original sin and restored to the supernatural order that was lost for all humankind by Adam. Only by grace, by the indwelling of the Holy Spirit, can the individual human person be reborn, justified, adopted, divinized, enabled to participate in the divine life, and elevated to the supernatural state. The very moment that the Holy Spirit begins to indwell an individual person, right here and right now in this earthly state of existence, the natural condition of that person is radically changed and he or she begins to live the supernatural life of grace. How this takes place, according to Augustine, is through baptism. While later theologians of the medieval and modern periods will contend that the grace of baptism may also be extended to an individual otherwise than through the physical pouring of water within the community of faith, the pattern of Augustine's thought will continue to hold sway throughout all subsequent Church history. The supernatural life is not reserved for heaven; it begins right here on earth, with baptism. We are reborn in baptism and changed from persons who live only a natural life into persons who simultaneously live the supernatural life of grace. Created in the image of God, through baptism we are recreated in the likeness of God as well.

As to the preternatural gifts, these, too, will be restored. Since we live simultaneously on the natural and the supernatural levels, grace does not obliterate the natural state of our humanity. Under the influence of grace, the effects of original sin are overcome, not all at once, but gradually. Little by little, freedom is rehabilitated, concupiscence mastered, harmony with creation restored, personal integrity reestablished, and human nature perfected. For most human beings, these preternatural gifts are not fully restored in this life. For all human beings, the last of these gifts, impassibility to suffering and bodily immortality, will not be restored in this life at all, but only in the afterlife of heaven.

Unless all these gifts are ultimately reestablished, the effects of Adam's sin would prove far more pervasive than those of Jesus' redemptive action. By elevating us to the supernatural life through grace and the indwelling of the Holy Spirit, indeed of the entire Trinity, Christ has guaranteed our immortality and pledged the full restoration of all the preternatural gifts. Even more, he has made it possible for us, who can do nothing on the level of created nature alone, to cooperate even in our own salvation and, on the supernatural level, to participate in the entire work of redemption. "To sum up, then," contrasting the effects of Adam's sin and Jesus' redemptive activity, St. Paul proclaims, "just as a single offense brought condemnation to all men, a single righteous act brought all men acquittal and life. Just as through one man's disobedience all became sinners, so through one man's obedience all shall become just" (Rom 5:18–19). In Christ, all that our first parents lost for us will be fully restored; and if, in fact, our first parents never did possess the full supernatural life, then the redemptive activity of Christ infinitely surpasses the effects of Adam's sin, for now the Trinity indwells us, grace elevates us, and even here we live the supernatural life.

Related Doctrines

The notion of the supernatural life is the heart and foundation of other significant doctrines of Catholicism. Among them, we will take a brief look at the incarnation of Jesus, sanctifying and created grace, merit and our participation in the salvific action of Christ, the immortality of the human soul, the final end of human beings, and the Marian doctrines of the Assumption and the Immaculate Conception. Each of these areas of Church teaching is directly related to the transformation of human beings in the supernatural order.

The Incarnation

Ever since the scholastic period there have been two opposing theological views on the necessity and purpose of the incarnation, and each view finds its relevancy in a particular understanding of the supernatural status of the human person. According to one position, the first human beings created by God already possessed the supernatural life, not as a quality of their created nature but as a gift of divine grace. Original sin, however, deprived them of this supernatural endowment and necessitated its restoration by a further act of divine generosity. As expressed by the Roman Liturgy, in words addressed to God the Father, "You came to our rescue by your power as God, but you wanted us to be saved by one like us. Man refused your friendship, but man himself was to restore it through Jesus Christ our Lord."[39] Although eternally foreseen by the Father, the incarnation was, therefore, a response to Adam's sin and the fall of human beings from grace. Without original sin, the incarnation of the Son of God would not have occurred. This was the position represented by St. Anselm and St. Thomas Aquinas in the scholastic period and by Walter Kasper today.[40]

The opposing position held that from the very beginning human beings were created with a disposition toward the supernatural life, but without its realization. Only through the conjoining of divinity and humanity would it be possible for human beings to fulfill their eternal destiny. Therefore, it was always in the divine plan, not merely by foreknowledge but by design, for the Son of God to become incarnate, thus making possible humankind's eternal destiny of supernatural communion with God. Jesus as the "new creation," the "new Adam," brought the destiny of all humanity to a fulfillment far superior to that of the first creation and the first Adam, but nonetheless intended from the very beginning. The incarnation, like grace itself, was not a divine afterthought in the wake of original sin. Rather it is the very presupposition for realizing humanity's highest destiny, the possibility of receiving the divine self-communication, God's very purpose in creating. Thus, even without the sin of Adam, the Son of God would have become incarnate, uniting divinity and humanity in the one person of Jesus Christ. In the scholastic period, this was the position developed by John Duns Scotus and promoted by his followers in the Franciscan school. Today it is advocated by an increasing number of contemporary theologians, among them Karl Rahner, Hans Urs von Balthasar, and Michael Schmaus.[41]

Both positions continue to be debated among Catholic theologians today, with, perhaps, the latter holding the edge among contemporary writers. Whichever position one were to adopt, however, the very possibility of union with God, the universal human significance of our adopted sonship in Christ, and the fulfillment of human personality and destiny in this world are all dependent upon the necessity of humanity's supernatural transformation. Otherwise, Jesus is reduced to an ethical teacher, a moral exemplar, an expositor of wisdom, and, at most, a divine sojourner on earth, while we human beings are left without any possibility of communion with God in this life and with only the vaguest notion of supernatural transformation in the next. On the other hand, the possibility of sharing in the sonship of Christ right now, the potential for divinization and participation in the very life of the Trinity at this moment, and the realization of that transcendence toward which we are all drawn by so many of our life experiences, these are only possible if, through our union with the incarnate Son of God, we have been truly transformed and given a share in the supernatural life. Without those possibilities being realized, the incarnation is only mythology and of no vital significance.

Sanctifying and Created Grace

The very notion of the incarnation came to dominate the teaching of the Fathers of the Church and awakened among them a strong belief in the supernatural life of graced human beings. True, they did not use the terms "supernatural life" or "grace." Rather, "divinization" was the term preferred by the Fathers of the Eastern Church, while "sanctification" became established in the vocabulary of the West. Yet, at the heart of patristic teaching there was always the conviction that the Holy Spirit indwells both the Church and the individual Christian. This indwelling of the Holy Spirit established the individual Christian's communion with God and affected his or her life and relationships in the world. This divine indwelling created a lasting and fundamental change in the life of a human being.

By the thirteenth century, scholastic theologians referred to this alteration in the Christian's life as an ontological change, since they understood it to be a fundamental and permanent alteration in the essential nature of the human person. The cause of this change was the indwelling of the Holy Spirit, and the primary effects were elevation to the supernatural state and a created capacity for right action, which they labeled "habitual" or "sanctifying grace." Because of the presence of sanctifying grace, the individual was saved from damnation, justified before God, enabled to receive innumerable other expressions of divine assistance known as "actual graces," and empowered to perform actions of a meritorious nature.

In the sixteenth century, Martin Luther denounced both the theology of the supernatural life and the notion of sanctifying grace as nothing more than inventions of scholastic theology. Using his principle of *sola scriptura* — only that is essential and worthy of belief which is clearly delineated in Scripture — he was unwilling to accept the notion of doctrinal development or the witness presented by patristic writings. While acknowledging the reality of divine indwelling, Luther denied that human beings were thereby elevated to the supernatural state, experienced an ontological change of a supernatural nature, or were empowered by sanctifying grace to perform meritorious acts. For Luther, grace does not elevate impaired human nature to a supernatural state. Rather, grace overrides the effects of a depraved human nature with the effects of Christ's redemptive death for us. We are not made just; we are declared to be just. God declares us to be just, based not on a divine gift of infused grace nor on grace-elevated good works of a meritorious nature, but solely on the extrinsic righteousness of Christ, which the sinner receives through faith alone. Thus, according to Luther, the Christian is *simul iustus et peccator* — at the same time both a just person and a sinner, one in whom both sin and grace coexist.

The difficulty with Luther's explanation is threefold. First of all, he separates sanctification from justification, thus allowing justifying grace to be operative on the level of basic human nature, where sanctification would not be possible. In Luther's view, one is not made just; one is simply accepted as just, and not because of one's own interior righteousness, but because of the extrinsic righteousness of Christ. Scholastic theology, on the other hand, viewed justification and sanctification as inseparably linked together; one cannot be justified without the action of sanctifying grace. Second, Luther overlooks the extensive patristic witness regarding divinization and sanctification, which the Fathers of the Church expounded in writings frequently documented with references to Sacred Scripture. Centuries before the development of scholastic theology, St. Augustine had already expounded on grace, its various types and effects (operative and cooperative, sufficient and efficient, prevenient and persevering). He also wrote about the relationship between grace and free will and, above all, about the deification of the human person by grace.[42] Third, Luther fails to offer a satisfying explanation for bridging the infinite gap between finite, limited human beings and God who is eternal and without limit.

In its simplest definition, justification is the process or action by which sinful, finite human beings come into union with an infinite and sinless God. Nothing in our created human nature provides for this. Nothing in created nature alone is capable of attaining it. By concentrating on the notion of justification, Luther emphasized bridging the gap between sinful human beings and sinless God. He did this by concentrating on the cross of Jesus. "For our sakes God made him who did not know sin to be sin, so that in him we might become the very holiness of God" (2 Cor 5:21). However, Luther failed to deal with the gap between God's infinity and humanity's finiteness. This is the question of sanctification. For Luther it was enough that a nature created and corrupted by concupiscence should experience simultaneously, but without elevation to the supernatural, the new creation of grace. One could be justified without being sanctified.

But how is that possible? How is it enough that God should declare a person just without also providing the means for holiness? Should there not be some alteration in the very order of creation itself, even an alteration foreseen, provided for, preplanned from the beginning of creation? To the Fathers of the Church this only made sense. How can that which is only natural come into contact with the supernatural, unless it is first brought into the realm of the supernatural? This was the question confronted by the

Fathers of the Church. They found the answer in the incarnation of Christ and the theology of divinization. Grace
accomplishes a real change in human beings. We are reborn,
justified, adopted, divinized, and given a share in the divine life. When the Son of God became a human being, a
marvelous exchange of natures at last became possible; the
human nature created for Christ was elevated by grace and
deified. In imitation of Christ and through the experience of
grace, every human being can now be deified, transformed,
and elevated to the supernatural life.[43]

Many contemporary theologians modify the scholastic
theology of sanctifying grace, but without deviating from
the doctrine of grace itself. By labeling as sanctifying grace
the created effect that takes place by the indwelling of the
Holy Spirit in the human person, the scholastics were prone
to speak of the loss of sanctifying grace by sin. Having
rightly emphasized the supernatural elevation and ontological change effected by grace, they found it more difficult to
explain how sanctifying grace could be lost by sin while the
supernatural elevation and ontological transformation remained unchanged, although inoperative for salvation. Most
often, contemporary theologians, rather than emphasizing
the created effects that take place when the Trinity indwells
a human person, prefer to speak of sanctifying grace as
the uncreated presence of the divine indwelling. Sanctifying grace is the very presence of God indwelling the human
person.

The first effect of that indwelling is the supernatural
transformation of the person, a transformation that cannot be reversed by sin, even if the divine indwelling itself
should be lost and the sanctifying effects of grace should
be surrendered through deliberate sinful actions of sufficient

seriousness. Thus, sanctifying grace, the divine indwelling, establishes the supernatural elevation of the human person. Created graces, on the other hand, are related to the supernatural state. They either prepare the human person for divine indwelling (prevenient grace), assist the human person in living the supernatural life and in dealing with all the exigencies of daily living (actual graces), or aid the human person in remaining faithful to the supernatural life received (persevering grace). Regardless of how one defines and categorizes grace, however, the truth arrived at by the Fathers of the Church during Christianity's infancy remains unaltered: without elevation to the supernatural life, for us there would be no grace.

Merit

In rejecting the scholastic teaching on grace, Luther's principal concern was to discredit the notion of merit and the increase of grace through human activity. Luther correctly understood the scholastic axiom: meritorious actions require elevating grace. Were he to have accepted the notion of the supernatural elevation of human beings by grace, he would have had to accept the notion of merit, for sanctifying grace makes meritorious action possible. Generally, theologians agree with Luther that, on the basis of created human nature, we can merit nothing. Our finite human actions cannot merit an infinite reward. Were we to accept the notion of merit based on human nature alone, we would find ourselves denying two of the basic tenets of Christian faith, namely, the full efficacy of Jesus' saving action and the absolute gratuity of God's grace. The efficacy of Jesus' once-for-all act of reconciliation should not require additional acts of reconciliation.

This does not deny, however, the need for human beings to appropriate to themselves the saving grace of Christ, nor the experience of transformation, of growing ever more deeply aware of one's stance before God. This cannot happen on the basis of created human nature alone. Elevated to the supernatural state, however, we can appropriate the supernatural grace of Christ and grow more deeply aware of our relationship with our Triune God. The complete gratuity of God's grace renders unnecessary, even prohibits, any meritorious activity by an individual person acting out of inherent human nature. The supernatural state, however, is a second nature added to the first, a totally gratuitous gift of God over and above inherent human nature. Any action of a human being in cooperation with God on the supernatural level necessarily remains an act of grace and does not violate the absolute gratuity of God's grace.

The entire Catholic notion of merit is based, therefore, not on the created nature of human beings, but on the free gift of supernatural life, fully the result of Jesus' salvific action and entirely a gratuitous gift of divine grace. The supernatural life is entirely God's gift; we can do nothing to earn it, and entrance into it is possible solely in light of the incarnation of the divine Son as a distinct man among human beings. Thus, Luther was correct in asserting that on the sole basis of created human nature, a person is incapable of meriting anything from God. However, elevated to the supernatural life, one enters into a realm of cooperation with Christ where merit itself is an act of divine grace. In short, merit is possible — not on the natural level of human activity, but on the supernatural level of grace.

Immortality

The doctrines of the immortality of the human person and of humanity's final destiny united with God in heaven, or separated from God in hell, are likewise dependent on the notion of the supernatural. Over the centuries the teaching of theologians, and of the Church itself, has not always been consistent and clear when attempting to explain the basis for the immortality of the human person or the destiny of the unbaptized individual. Like human beings, other living creatures are identified as having souls, yet the souls of living creatures other than humans have never been seriously considered as candidates for eternal life. If our first parents, and all those after them until Jesus entered on the stage of world history, did not share in the supernatural life and possessed only human souls in their natural created state, why should the human soul be any more immortal than that of any other creature on earth? If, on the other hand, our first parents were created in the supernatural state prior to the impairment of sin (or at least with an additional God-gifted disposition for the supernatural life, such as Rahner's theory of the "supernatural existential" proposes to support), then the immortality of the human person is assured and only one's final destiny remains in question — union with God or separation from God.

All of this, of course, remains speculation for philosophers and theologians, very much like the question of the final destiny of the unbaptized person — confined to hell, stranded in limbo, transformed at death, instantaneously enlightened, simply annihilated, or any number of other conceivable possibilities. Setting philosophical speculation aside, however, the doctrine of Christianity handed down from the patristic era is clear: the human person who has been reborn in baptism and supernaturally transformed by indwelling grace is immortal and possesses an eternal destiny. Immortality and eternal life are certainties only in light of the supernatural state, assured for us in baptism.

Marian Doctrines

The Fathers of the Second Vatican Council devoted the final chapter of *Lumen Gentium,* the Dogmatic Constitution on the Church, to the role of the Blessed Virgin Mary, the Mother of God, in the mystery of Christ and the Church. The particular insight of this chapter was the Council Fathers' recognition of Mary as the first follower of Christ, the first Christian as it were, the first member of the Church. From the earliest days of Christianity, the Church of both the East and the West honored Mary with special devotion and found in her dedication to Christ the model of our dedication as well. The local churches of the East and the West today continue to honor Mary in a way prototypical for all Christians. Mary was the first one to receive the incarnate word of God. She was the first one to carry that incarnate word to others. She stands as the first witness of the signs and sayings of her son, the first to experience the full significance of his crucifixion, and among the first to receive the Holy Spirit sent from the Father at Pentecost. Everything that is said of Mary may also, in some way, be said of us, fellow members with her in the Church founded in Christ.

Only the Catholic Church has formally defined two of the significant Marian doctrines, the Immaculate Conception and the Assumption. In each definition, however, the norm stated above holds true. What is said of Mary, the first Christian, is said of us as well. When the Church declares that Mary was conceived without original sin in order to enter fully into the mystery of Christ, the Church also declares that we Christians are reborn in the waters of baptism, reborn free from original sin, in order to enter fully into that same Christological mystery. When the Church proclaims that at death the entire person of Mary was taken into heaven, into that fullness of union with the Trinity which is within the divinely gifted capacity of a human being, the Church also proclaims that we Christians will be assumed as well into the fullness of heavenly glory if we have remained faithful to our baptismal call. The definitions of the Assumption and the Immaculate Conception are not so extraordinary as to exclude ordinary Christians from sharing in the same destiny as the Mother of Jesus. The key to understanding the Assumption and the Immaculate Conception is the same key that unlocks the mysteries of baptism and eternal life, namely, the supernatural state into which all Christians enter through the mediation of the Church, the supernatural life which we live even here, even now, this side of heaven.

Implications for an Applied Theology

Moral Consequences

Some significant implications arise from this notion of our entering the supernatural life even here, in this world, as we live out our natural earthly existence. Since we live simultaneously on two levels, the natural and the supernatural, the first of these implications is that everything we do may have eternal consequences. Decisions made, actions performed, and thoughts consciously conceived may all bear eternal significance. Very often this is not something that our contemporaries want to hear. Often we may not want to hear it ourselves. There was a time, and not so long ago, when people were very conscious that their daily actions and decisions could well impact their eternal destiny. The question of heaven or hell was considered a pressing concern. Unfortunately, when approached obsessively, this notion often led to anxiety about living and fear of dying. Seemingly enlightened individuals, therefore, chose to put the question behind them and to go on living as though their actions had no consequence beyond the immediate and the apparent. This has not led to healthy and balanced living, however, as Dr. Karl Menninger pointed out in his now famous book, *Whatever Became of Sin?*[44] Healthy, balanced living requires us to acknowledge the consequences of our actions, just as it requires us to recognize our faults and our sins. The forethought and caution that arise from focusing on the possibly eternal consequences of our decisions need not lead to increased anxiety or unfounded fear. They should, however, lead us to a greater appreciation of the supernatural life we already live.

The Nature of Heaven

A second implication concerns the very nature of heaven itself. Far too many people tend to look upon heaven as the reward for living a good life on earth. This whole notion is problematic for several reasons. It leads an individual to believe that he or she is earning the way to eternal life, convinced that in exchange for living a good life on this earth, God owes that person a place in heaven. It leads to fear that a single fall from grace may dash the hopes of an entire life-time of conscientious living. It leads to resentment that the last-minute convert from sin should inherit the same heaven that the righteous person has earned by a lifetime of trying to avoid sin altogether. It fails to recognize that living right-eously is a response to grace, not the achievement of personal effort. It creates a great mental chasm between heaven and earth, as if none of the gifts of heaven are available to us until we cross over the great divide of death. Finally, it makes life burdensome and death fearful — God is in heaven, but the world is a treacherous place.

Recognizing that the supernatural life begins for us right now changes the whole concept of heaven. Heaven is not the reward for living a good life on earth; heaven is the comple-tion of the grace-filled life already lived. God is not waiting for us in heaven; God is with us right now on earth — and the world is filled with signs of God's presence. Living righteously now brings with it the joy of already sharing God's life. Not that living in this world is unadulterated joy, that we could possibly live without the experience of disappointment, frailty, or sorrow, but that heaven will be the completion and fullness of the joy and grace we have already experienced, as well as the elimination of every-thing that has ever separated us from God. The Kingdom of Heaven is already in our midst because even here we live the supernatural life.

The Incompleteness of Life

Yet, we cannot deny that we do not yet experience the full-ness of God's Kingdom. In fact, we live in a state of existence between the "already" and the "not yet," between the Kingdom of God already in our midst and the Kingdom not yet fully realized, between heaven already begun and heaven not yet complete, between grace already experienced and sin not yet fully conquered. This is the third implication of already living the supernatural life: it is not complete, nor are we, and so we owe it to ourselves to be patient and to look for the signs of God's life already present in ourselves and in our world. It is true that humankind's original sin somehow involved the loss of the preternatural gifts intended for us by God and that these gifts are not yet fully restored. Nonetheless, while we have already begun to live the supernatural life itself, we anticipate the day when all the preternatural gifts — freedom from persistent concupiscence, bodily immortality, physical impassibility, harmony with creation, personal integrity, and complete happiness — will be ours in the full realization of God's Kingdom; and so we continue to live in this passing world with our hearts set on the world that will never end — but a world that has, nonetheless, already begun.

Response to Grace

The final implication to be mentioned here is this: living already the supernatural life should help us to realize that our every good act is a response to grace. Augustine and Aquinas, like so many theologians before and after them, debated the question of natural good acts. Is any human being capable of performing a single act of goodness that is not a response to grace, or are human beings so lost in depravity and so centered on themselves that even what appears to be an act of goodness is really performed for less laudatory motives? Such thinking might well make us suspicious of our own good actions and paranoid about those of others. Explaining the quality of goodness in the actions of those who have not yet entered into the supernatural life is a challenge for philosophy and theology to deal with. For those who recognize their rebirth to eternal life, however, in the characteristic phrase of St. Therese of Lisieux, "All is grace."[45] All the good that we do is not so much our doing as it is God's doing. We are only responding to God's prompting in our souls. We can no more earn our way into the supernatural state than we can rebirth ourselves. The supernatural life is entirely God's gift; therefore every act of goodness that flows from the supernatural life remains God's gift as well. All the good that we do is but our cooperation with what God has chosen to do in us and through us. We are only responding to him. There is great liberation in knowing this. Even greater is the challenge to search out and recognize how God is active in our lives. We do not need to wait for heaven to know Christ, his Father, and the Spirit. The Kingdom of God is already in our midst because even here we live the supernatural life.

Chapter 3

"God Respects
Our Human Freedom"

In his entertaining collection of stories entitled *Lake Wobegon Days*,[46] humorist Garrison Keillor relates the arrival in town of Brother Bob and Sister Verna, "Bible-thumping evangelists" according to his description. They have come to preach "the Revival," and they arrive in a white van covered with hundreds of abbreviated Bible verses. The passages are not professionally painted and are, perhaps, even a bit difficult to read, causing fellow travelers and passersby to stare and squint at them in an attempt to decipher what is written. No doubt recipients of a mail order preacher's license, Bob and Verna have taken to heart their ministry to proclaim the Gospel along the highways and the byways, leaving no stone unturned and no individual unapproached with the offer of salvation. Once people have seen the van and scanned even one of its messages, they can't argue that they never heard the Gospel or that it was never preached to them. If they fail to accept the word of God, repent of their sins, and reform their lives, they have no one to blame but themselves, and they have no excuse to hide behind on judgment day. They have been offered amazing grace, and if they refuse it they have only damnation to look forward to. Bob and Verna, on the other hand, have done their job and avoided the injunction of God:

If I say to the wicked man, You shall surely die, and you do not warn him or speak out to dissuade him from his wicked conduct so that he may live: the wicked man shall die for his sin, but I will hold you responsible for his death. If, on the other hand, you have warned the wicked man, yet he has not turned away from his evil nor from his wicked conduct, then he shall die for his sin, but you shall save your life. (Ezek 3:18–19)

It is probably this same manner of thinking that inspires the signs "John 3:16" that appear among the spectators at professional sporting events all across the country: "God so loved the world that he gave his only Son, that whoever believes in him may not die but may have eternal life." These banners and posters and hand-held signs are meant to challenge the reader to accept Jesus as his or her savior, and they allow the bearer to take credit for proclaiming the Gospel and witnessing to faith. Would that preaching the Gospel and securing the offer of salvation were so easy. Would that the mere circulation of the written Gospel text were enough to bring people to faith, or that reading the words of Scripture provided a sufficient basis for accepting Jesus or rejecting him altogether.

The reality is that we humans are complex beings composed of flesh and spirit, intellection and volition, feelings and affections. In order to make fully human decisions — for or against anything — we need clarity of understanding and freedom of will. Yet very often we short-circuit the entire process, pass judgments, and make decisions for entirely wrong reasons and on very insufficient grounds. We are quite capable of getting so wrapped up at any one level of our complex personalities that we fail to understand the realities that confront us or the consequences of what we decide. At any one moment, our current disposition may open us to see the full picture and to make a proper decision with clarity and freedom, or our momentary disposition is just as likely to prohibit us from achieving sufficient understanding and an uninhibited exercise of free will. We all share the experience, at one time or another, of failing to hear what another person has said, no matter how clearly and emphatically he or she said it, simply because, at that moment, we were not prepared to hear it or disposed to accept it. It is no different when God speaks to us. If we are not disposed to listen to God and to hear what God is saying, we are not capable, at that moment, of understanding God's word or accepting what God has said. Yet God made us this way, and God respects what God has made.

Beginning with Scripture, but certainly crystallized in the teaching of the Church Fathers, there was a fundamental belief that God does not force the divine will on anyone. Rather, God offers God's word and God's presence to us and, through our free will, makes it possible for us to receive what God has offered. This is true of God's grace, of God's revelation, even of the advent of God's own Son, who "came to his own, yet whose own did not accept him" (John 1:11). When humankind fell into sin and away from God, becoming "like slaves subordinated to the elements of the world," as St. Paul argues, God did not abandon the people God had created. Rather, God continued to send prophets and teachers for their instruction and guidance. Finally, "when the designated time had come, God sent forth his Son born of a woman, born under the law, to deliver from the law those who were subjected to it, so that we might receive our status as adopted sons" (Gal 4:3–5). Still, God did not force acceptance of the Son. Rather, God respected the freedom given to the people God had created and allowed them to make a decision for Christ or against him. In the words of the Gospel of John, however, "Any who did accept him he empowered to become the children of God" (John 1:12).

Throughout the Gospels, Jesus extends the invitation to follow him, but he does not coerce acceptance of that invitation. Perhaps the most famous illustration of this is found in the story of the rich young man in the Gospel of Matthew. Seeking greater perfection than he had found in scrupulously maintaining all the Jewish laws, the young man sought out Jesus and asked his advice. In response, Jesus invited him to sell all his worldly possessions and join the company of disciples. Hearing this, the young man went away sad, for his possessions were many and he was too much attached to them. Because of his wealth, the young man was not disposed to accept Jesus' invitation. No doubt saddened by the young man's response, Jesus allowed him to depart but warned his disciples about too much attachment to worldly things (Matt 19:16–26). This passage illustrates not only the danger of riches, but also the freedom which is ours to accept and follow Christ. It is noteworthy that Jesus does not condemn the young man for his choice. He does not say that it is impossible for him to enter heaven. Rather, he comments on the difficulty that attachment to wealth imposes on those seeking admission to the Kingdom of God, and he implies, with hope, that God will continue to extend the invitation. "For man it is impossible; for God all things are possible."

The Fathers of the Church were likewise convinced that God respects our human freedom despite the evil that often results from our unfortunate choices. Moreover, God does not impose God's will on us, but continues to invite our response. Against the Gnostics who claimed that some individuals are enlightened by special divine knowledge that overrides their free will in the election of good, St. Irenaeus adamantly professed that God endows all human beings with the same freedom, so that they might voluntarily choose good, avoid evil, and come to recognize how magnanimous God truly is.[47] Earlier in the same work, Irenaeus had illustrated the noble generosity of God by demonstrating how, through the long centuries of human history, God had even allowed for the misuse of freedom in the commission of sin so that human beings might also learn by experience the evil from which they have been delivered by Christ and freely express their gratitude to him.[48] "God made man free from the beginning," Irenaeus wrote, "so that he possessed his proper power just as he possessed his own soul, to follow the will of God freely, not being compelled by Him. With God there is no coercion."[49]

St. Clement of Alexandria expressed the common belief of the Fathers that a willing disposition on our part is more in keeping with God's plan than would be the imposition of the divine will on us: "To save the unwilling is to exercise compulsion; but to save the willing belongs to the One who bestows grace."[50] In a final note from the Fathers, St. Augustine testifies to their belief that the human person cannot respond to the call of God unless correctly disposed and properly open to receive it. "There are those chosen," he wrote, "who respond to God's call, but there are also those who do not respond to the call and, therefore, do not obey it. In the end, even though they were called, these are not chosen because they did not respond."[51] In a similar vein he continues, "Men are moved to faith, one in one way, one in another. The same thing said to two persons may move one and not the other, while the same thing said to a person on one occasion may move him, yet when said on another occasion it may not."[52] When we are properly disposed to God, we are able to hear God's call and respond to it. When the proper dispositions are absent, however, we can neither hear nor respond. Much has been written about the source and cause of our proper dispositions, but the bottom line is that we can receive only what we are disposed to receive.

Almost from its inception, the Church found itself locked in conflict with the dual heresies of Gnosticism and Docetism. The common element in these two heresies is that both denied the value of the material world in God's communication with human beings. Both saw created matter as an obstacle and a threat to the voice of the spirit. Gnosticism held that the truth that sets humankind free was not knowledge derived through human senses and human reasoning. Rather, it was an infused enlightenment that came directly to human understanding by a type of divine intervention. This knowledge was not available to all people, but only to a select few chosen directly by God. Much later, drawing on the teaching of the pagan philosopher Aristotle, St. Thomas Aquinas would convincingly argue that there is no knowledge available to the human mind that does not come by way of the senses, either for apprehension or for comprehension. Nothing exists in our consciousness that we have not first experienced by the senses. Even infused knowledge, which is not beyond God's activity in human life, requires a body of knowledge already acquired by the senses in order to be interpreted and understood.[53] Theologians today speak of the importance of analogical knowledge for the comprehension of divine truth. Without the use of analogical thinking, we cannot relate the truths of God to the human capacity for understanding, for the truths of God always lie infinitely beyond human comprehension.[54] The ability to think analogically comes from the foundation of knowledge acquired by way of the senses and made the object of reflection. In the apprehension of divine truth, we can receive only what we, by our innate human nature, are disposed to receive.

Docetism also sought to bypass created materiality as the medium of God's communication with us. Gnosticism was largely concerned with the manner in which God communicates the word of revelation to the human mind. Docetism went a step further by focusing its attention on how the Word of God, the divine logos, the Son of the Father, entered into the world to communicate the presence of God directly to humankind. Docetism denied any true incarnation. Christ assumed a human body but did not become a human being. His human nature, his life, and his sufferings were not real but only apparent. According to the Docetists, a real incarnation would be degrading to the divine nature since materiality was, in itself, degraded. As a result, any true communication with Christ and any true knowledge of God could come about only in the realm of the spirit, only in the contact of human spirit with divine spirit, and never through a real connection between the material and the spiritual.

Many people, even today, remain Docetists at heart. While they love and reverence the stories of Jesus in Scripture, their mind's eye always sees the divine nature of Jesus at work in his miracles, as though somehow, even here on earth, his divinity remained separated from his human appearance. Jesus was God walking around in a human body. God was present in Jesus, but somehow the divinity remained invisibly distinct from his visible human form. It is God who cured the sick, healed the deaf, raised the dead, opened the eyes of the blind.

The humanity of Jesus was reduced to a somewhat defective vehicle of God's action, to be left behind when Jesus rose from the tomb. In prayer, it is to the divinity of Jesus that they address their prayers, confident that because he once experienced our human frailty, he will lend a sympathetic ear; but it is not his humanity they invoke in prayer. According to such thinking, it is in the spirit that we are saved, not in the flesh. Such thinking fails to realize that it is through our flesh that God communicates with our spirit. It is the inheritance of Docetism still present with us. As beings of spirit and matter, however, we can receive only what our incarnate human nature disposes us to receive.

The scholastic theologians of a later generation restated this idea in a formula that every seminary student in the past committed to memory — *Quidquid recipitur ad modum recipientis recipitur.* "Whatever is received is received according to the mode of the receiver." The limitation implicit in this notion is that we can receive only what our limited human nature permits us to receive. On the other hand, it is our created human nature that permits us to communicate with the divine spirit of God.[55] In this, we, of all God's creatures, can take glory. Since, within our innate nature we experience the communication of flesh and spirit, then it is through the flesh of our incarnate nature that our spirits can communicate with the very spirit of God. This is the basis for the sacramental principle so largely identified with Catholic Christianity — that God communicates grace to us through the created materiality of our world. Because we are beings of flesh and spirit, God always communicates with us in an incarnational manner. Bound by our materiality, we enter into communication with God, not by infused knowledge, but through the material world and natural signs, through God's creation and through nature itself. It is the incarnational principle that we see in operation when God communicates revelation to us, when the divine Second Person of the Trinity became incarnate as Jesus of Nazareth, and when the sacraments of the Church are celebrated in our communities and in our lives. The incarnational principle and the sacramental principle are the same.

Materiality is the mode of our reception. To comprehend God's communication requires our ability to reflect upon the world around us. According to a Catholic understanding, all revelation, creation included, is, therefore, incarnational. The promise of God is made not only in words, but is accompanied by physical signs and attached to material substances, as well. God speaks to us in burning bushes and pillars of fire, in bread that is broken and wine poured out, in water that cleanses and oil that heals, in words that are first proclaimed and then written down, in the imagery of shepherds and servants and a woman in search of a lost coin. Materiality is the mode of our reception because this is the only way that we can receive what God communicates to us.

To receive God's communication in all its varied forms is no easy matter. It doesn't happen by osmosis. It doesn't happen without our active engagement and total cooperation. True, human beings do take in most sensations and impressions and a great deal of information on the level of the subconscious. Artists and poets, including the artist and the poet in each one of us, often surface these impressions in a manner mysterious even to themselves. Others often find in the artists' work impressions and ideas of which they themselves were seemingly unaware, but which were, nonetheless, the product of their own subconscious minds. The viewer or the reader who strives to completely understand and, thereby, totally receive what has been presented is often more conscious of the notions expressed than is the artist or poet. Full reception, however, requires full comprehension. The degree to which we receive anything depends upon the degree of our comprehension, and comprehension depends upon our dispositions, on those things which affect our ability and willingness to receive. This is even more critical where it is God's grace and self-communication that is the object of our receiving.

There are many dispositions that affect our ability to receive what God seeks to communicate to us. These dispositions often vary from situation to situation — how alert or distracted we may be, how well we feel, how others around us divert or focus our attention, the mood we are in, or the manner in which something is expressed. Aside from these, there are three essential dispositions that must always be present for reception to take place — knowledge, faith, and advertence. Knowledge, in this case, is more than awareness, and it is more than simply knowing what others think to be so. This knowledge is the conviction that I know something is so. Without such knowledge, reception cannot take place. Accompanying such knowledge is faith, the conviction that what I know to be so is, in fact, valuable and intended for me. It is the conviction that God's promise is reliable, that I can depend upon God's word and God's favor. Without such faith, true reception cannot take place. Advertence follows upon knowledge and faith. To advert is to pay attention or give heed. I must be fully attentive to what God intends to do for me and I must give heed to God's action in my life. Such advertence involves both acknowledging through prayer and thanksgiving what God intends to do for me and putting

God's gifts to work in my life. To pronounce gratitude is not enough; I must demonstrate my gratitude by attentively making use of God's gift. Without such advertence, full reception cannot take place.

A mundane example, not at all religious in nature, may help to clarify these ideas. Should a benefactor unknown to yourself make a large deposit to your bank account without having notified you, your account would be larger but you could hardly be said to have received the increase, since you do not know it is there. Without knowing about it, you can do nothing with it, and, so, you have not yet received it. When your monthly statement arrives, however, you note the increase. Still, your first thought is that some mistake has been made. You can't believe the money is really yours, even when the teller assures you that the deposit was correctly made. You cannot even spend the money without the fear that a mistake will be discovered and you will have to repay what you spent. Once you hear from your benefactor, however, and are assured that the money is really yours to spend, you have the necessary confidence to truly receive what has been given. One step remains, however, for reception to be complete: you must acknowledge the gift that has been made. A note or word of thanks may seem to suffice, but real acknowledgment takes place when you begin to make use of the gift that has been given. At last, full reception takes place. The dispositions of the receiver are essential for full reception.

We must know, we must believe, and we must act, consciously and reflectively, upon God's gift, whatever it may be, in order to fully receive it. Even God's grace and favor, then, are received according to the disposition of the receiver, according to our ability and willingness to receive. Because we are beings of flesh and spirit, because God respects what God has created, because God does not force the divine will on anyone, and because we are allowed to be free, for all these reasons, this notion rings true: we can receive only what we are disposed to receive.

Related Doctrines

Several significant Church doctrines are directly related to this notion that the dispositions of the recipient play a decisive role in a person's reception of God's self-communication in grace and revelation. Our attention will focus on three of these doctrines, namely, inspiration, the nature and reception of the sacraments, and the effectiveness of sacramental absolution. Within each of these doctrines there is a clear understanding that God does not force the divine will on anyone. Rather, God offers the gift of divine presence and assistance and leaves each individual free to respond. In the freedom of that response, the relationship between God and the individual human person is deepened and finds its most profound expression. God could have created human beings with a requisite condition of responding in obedience to the divine will. Instead, humankind was created to respond in freedom to the divine invitation. In such freedom one's very relationship with God is discovered, for without freedom, relationship is impossible.

Inspiration

Although revelation is necessarily linked with divine inspiration, inspiration itself is concerned with neither the subject nor the object of divine revelation. It is not concerned with the nature of God who reveals, nor with the data that has been revealed by God. Rather, inspiration refers to the medium of divine revelation and to the manner in which God communicates to us the divine presence, truth, and grace.

The mechanism of divine inspiration is essentially linked to the inspiration of the poet and the artist, to what is often referred to as the "poetic imagination." Artistic inspiration works upon the subconscious of the human mind that constantly gathers in impressions of which the conscious mind is unaware. It works upon the natural disposition of a human mind attuned to dealing with images, symbols, and fleeting sensations. Reflecting in tranquility or under the pressure of heightened emotion, the human mind conceives new ideas from the synthesis of impressions rising to consciousness. Perhaps without full comprehension of the meaning to be expressed, it is, nonetheless, the conscious mind that converts the artist's impressions to canvas or paper or musical notation. The artist may feel overtaken by the creative muse, yet it is the conscious mind that ultimately gives order to impressions and translates them into a medium of artistic communication. Drawing from the reservoir of his or her talents, responding to interior dispositions, and utilizing skills honed through experience, the artist responds consciously to inspiration and produces a work of art. The artist may not fully comprehend all that he or she has depicted. Further reflection may reveal more than that of which he or she was first aware. Individual observers, the artist included, may respond simply on the affective level to the beauty of what has been created without any true conscious understanding. Yet the meaning can be received and fully appreciated only on the level of conscious reflection.

In the same way, God inspires the human person by flooding the subconscious mind with symbols, images, and impressions, working on the natural dispositions of the human person to bring about synthesis and order and to draw the whole mental conception to the level of the conscious idea. Perhaps the Fathers of the Second Vatican Council came closest to defining divine inspiration when speaking of the manner in which the believer assents in faith to that which God has revealed. "If this faith is to be shown, the grace of God and the interior help of the Holy Spirit must precede and assist, moving the heart and turning it to God, opening the eyes of the mind, and giving 'joy and ease to everyone in assenting to the truth and believing it.' To bring about an ever deeper understanding of revelation, the same Holy Spirit constantly brings faith to completion by His gifts."[56]

Thus, inspiration is the action of divine grace working interiorly on the human mind, bringing to conscious understanding that which the subconscious mind conceals. It is a process of grace that is fully compatible with the incarnate nature of the human person, comprised of flesh and spirit. It responds to the sacramental principle by which God speaks to us through the world of material creation and leads us by grace to discover the divine presence and self-communication. It recognizes the nature of the human mind that is entrapped or liberated by the dispositions of the heart. Divine inspiration does not overtake the human person but works through the natural dispositions of each individual, recognizing that we can receive only what we are disposed to receive.

Sacraments

God speaks to us in many and varied ways, in particular through the community of faith, through the word of Scripture broken open for our understanding, and through the sacraments of the Church.

The Gospel of Luke presents these three realities in the wondrous passage about the two disciples making their way from Jerusalem to Emmaus on the afternoon of Jesus' resurrection (Lk 24:13–35). Disconsolate at the death of Jesus and unable to believe in his resurrection, Cleopas and his companion are journeying home. They are joined by a stranger whom they do not recognize as being Jesus himself. The stranger attempts to console them in their sorrow by recounting for them all the passages of Scripture referring to the death of the messiah. Reaching their village, they invite him into their house, but it is not until he blesses and breaks the bread with them that they realize that this stranger was Jesus all along. From that moment, they can no longer see him with their eyes of flesh but only through the eyes of faith.

The message of Luke is clear: in our journey through life, from Jerusalem to Emmaus, Jesus walks with us. He is with us in the company of his disciples, for wherever two or three of us are gathered in his name, he is in our company as well. He is with us whenever the pages of Scripture are proclaimed and interpreted for our understanding. He is with us in the sacraments, in the "breaking of the bread," the earliest Christian reference to the Eucharist. Invisible to human sight, he remains visible to the eyes of faith. Jesus is truly risen and ascended to the Father, but since his resurrection, we can still discover his presence in the community of the Church, in the proclamation of Scripture, and in the celebration of the sacraments.

Sacraments are not magical acts. They do not produce grace like a magician pulling a rabbit from a hat or a coin from thin air. Mere attendance at the sacramental liturgy does not assure participants the reception of grace. At the same time, the Church testifies that every sacramental enactment is effective of grace.[57] The solution to this seeming contradiction is quite simple. Sacraments bestow grace according to the promise of God, but that grace can be received solely according to the dispositions of the receiver. The first recipient of every sacrament is the Church itself, the Church which, despite the defects of individual members, is always holy because Christ, whose body the Church is, and the Spirit, who indwells the Church, themselves are holy. Therefore, the grace of sacramental action that comes forth from the promise of the Father is always received by Church, as well as by those individual members who share the dispositions proper for reception.

Sacraments are signs of God's promise. They bestow grace according to the intention of the giver, who is God. The medieval scholastic theologians expressed this notion in the dictum *ex opere operato*. Sacraments bestow grace "according to the intention of the giver." In all the sacraments, God uses natural gifts and signs, not just spoken words but material signs, to communicate meaning beyond what words alone can express. Such signs appeal to our created human nature, respecting the manner in which we experience the world and arrive at faith. Through water, oil, bread and wine, human touch and human symbol we are led from the natural to the supernatural, from the immanent to the transcendent. Our very nature as incarnate spirit is

the precondition for our encounter through created materiality with transcendent divinity. Beyond words, heart speaks
to heart, God to us and we to God. God communicates
Godself in real signs, that is, in signs that communicate not
merely mental images and intellectual meaning, but the very
reality that they symbolize. Water truly cleanses from sin,
human touch transfers divine power, bread and wine become the real presence of Christ himself. Such signs must
be reflected upon to be understood. For our part, they require faith that God, who has promised to communicate
grace through material signs, is always faithful to that promise — *ex opere operato,* according to the intention of the
giver.

To be fully effective in our individual lives, to bestow on
us their entire complement of grace, the sacraments not only
must be given by God but they must be received by us as
well. Such reception depends upon our dispositions, our ability and readiness to receive the grace that is offered. The
medieval scholastic theologians expressed this notion in the
dictum *ex opere operantis.* The grace of the sacraments is
received "according to the disposition of the receiver." The
first receiver of every sacrament is, of course, the Church,
the community of believers. Each member of the community
shares in the graced dispositions of the entire Church, but
only to the degree that one is, in fact, a member. This is particularly important for the reception of certain sacraments
when the personal dispositions of the individual receiver
may not be apparent or functional. Infant baptism and the
anointing of unconscious persons come readily to mind. The
Eastern Church practice of Chrismation and the giving of the
Eucharist to newly baptized children are further examples.
Even in these cases, however, the *full reception* of sacramen-

tal grace depends on the development of mature dispositions within the recipient.

In the case of those sacraments which admit of frequent reception or depend on greater maturity on the part of the recipients, the immediate and personal dispositions of the receiver are especially significant. The basic dispositions are knowledge, faith, and advertence. To receive the grace of Christ, we must know what he has promised, have faith that what he said is true, and advert to his presence in our lives. It is not enough to know what others believe about the sacraments; I must know it for myself with the certainty that arises from moral conviction. It is not enough to believe that God can bestow grace through material signs; I must myself believe that God bestows grace on me through sacramental signs, that I am included in God's promise. It is not enough to want to receive God's grace through sacramental participation; I must be attentive and open and committed to putting God's grace to work in my life. Without such dispositions, I cannot attain the grace that God offers and that must be received by me.

The Efficacy of Absolution

During the medieval scholastic period, heated theological debate occurred over the issue of what actually caused the forgiveness of sins in the sacrament of penance. The "contritionists," who included St. Anselm, Peter Lombard, and St. Albert the Great, held that the contrition of the penitent effected the forgiveness of sins. For these theologians, absolution by the priest was considered to be either the declaration by the Church that God had already taken away a person's sins, or the prayer of the Church petitioning God for forgiveness of the penitent. There was also a clear understanding that the sacramental encounter might well be the occasion and experience that would bring the penitent to true contrition. Opposed to the contritionists were the "absolutionists," whose numbers included Bl. John Duns Scotus, St. Bonaventure, and St. Thomas Aquinas. These theologians held that priestly absolution itself effected the forgiveness of sins. The contrition of the penitent was understood to be a necessary disposition for the reception of the grace of forgiveness immediately effected by absolution.

It would be nearly three hundred years before the Council of Trent would definitely settle this debate by declaring absolution to be the direct and immediate cause for the forgiveness of sins within the sacrament of penance.[58] At the same time, the Council declared that contrition, confession, and satisfaction are necessary dispositions for the reception of the sacrament and that, even outside the sacrament of penance, "the disposition of contrition is necessary at all times for the attainment of the remission of sins."[59] Within the sacrament of penance, the Council declared, imperfect contrition is a sufficient disposition to receive the grace of forgiveness effected by absolution.[60] God has promised the forgiveness of sins through the sacrament of penance. To receive that grace, however, mere participation in the ritual is insufficient. One must have knowledge, faith, and advertence — a conscious resolve to abandon sin and live in the grace of reconciliation. The ritual itself cannot forgive. Going through the motions will not suffice. One must be resolved — to the best of one's ability — not to sin again. Contrition, confession, and satisfaction are necessary dispositions for the penitent. Absolution assures that the grace of reconciliation is available to the penitent who is properly disposed, but we can receive only what we are disposed to receive.

Implications for an Applied Theology

How God communicates with us in every dimension of grace, revelation, and personal presence is based on what we are — incarnate spirit, *Geist im Welt,* spirit in the world.[61] From this predisposition of immanence and transcendence, of flesh and spirit, a number of other dispositions are derived which open or close the individual at any particular moment to a fuller or less full apprehension of reality. We can receive only what we are prepared to receive by our innate nature or immediate disposition. From this notion several significant implications arise for living the Christian life. Three such implications involve the sacramental experience of creation, the nature of human freedom, and our reception of the Eucharist.

The Sacramental Experience of Creation

God's sole means of communication with us is through our created intelligence and through signs of the divine presence implanted within the materiality of our world. The sacraments of the Church awaken our sensibilities to the fact that God has always communicated with us through the world itself. In our search for the meaning of symbol, in our need to reach beyond the limitations of this earth, in our desire to transcend the inner structure of our own being, we rise to encounter God. Aside from the Old Testament psalmist, perhaps no poet has so well captured the sacramental nature of creation as did the English Jesuit Gerard Manley Hopkins, who lived in the latter half of the nineteenth century. He saw the whole world "charged with the grandeur of God," reflecting the divine light "like shining from shook foil." Even in the midst of the most bleak and sordid conditions and dehumanizing excesses of the industrial revolution, Hopkins envisioned nature as "never spent" and the divine Spirit as continuing to manifest itself in "the dearest freshness deep down things."[62]

There is a real danger in overintellectualizing faith, the danger of reducing belief to doctrinal formulas and creedal statements. Laws — whether of dogma, church discipline, or liturgical celebration — can be removed from their proper context, set out of balance, and given an ascendancy over faith that saps the life of the community of believers and the vigor of one's personal experience of God. The counterbalance is to develop a personal awareness of the sacramentality of creation itself, to find God's presence in the cosmos. In an earlier age of Church history, from the patristic era through the period of the great scholastics, theologians spoke not of two pillars of theology but of three, including nature alongside God and humanity.[63] These foundations of theology and personal belief might be compared to a farmer's milking stool: it's easier and more stable to sit on a three-legged stool than one with only two legs. With three legs you can keep your balance.

St. Thomas Aquinas found the study of God in the cosmos to be one of the essential pillars of theology. "God," he wrote, "brought things into being that the divine goodness might be communicated to creatures and be represented by them. Because the divine goodness could not be adequately represented by one creature alone, God produced many and diverse creatures, that what was lacking in one in the representation of divine goodness might be supplied by another." "The whole universe together," he continued, "participates in divine goodness more perfectly, and represents it more adequately, than any single creature could do."[64] After Aquinas's time, the cosmos as the third pillar of theology began to fade from view. In time it nearly disappeared. We should reclaim it. Material creation is meant to lead us to the God who is both immanent and transcendent. The very nature of the human person predisposes us to this vision. To find signs of God in the material cosmos, to search for God who transcends creation — these are proper tasks for human beings. They match how we are made: spirit in the world.

Freedom

One of the basic dispositions of the human person is freedom, for in defining human nature, a sense of freedom is intimately linked with the desire for transcendence. Both freedom and transcendence allow us to escape our personal limitations and rise above ourselves. We are created by God to be free and to experience true liberty. Often, however, we confuse freedom or liberty with the power of choice, as if the license and ability to choose between two or more objects was enough to make us free. It is true that such "freedom of choice" may create within us a feeling of liberation, but, in fact, where true liberty exists, the power of choice may well cease to exist. Since real freedom comes from the ability to know what is truly good and the liberation to be able to choose it, when that which is truly good presents itself, the free person can choose nothing else. Were we to know clearly and certainly that which is truly good but, at the same moment, be unable to choose it, we would not be free at all. We would be under constraint.

St. Augustine discovered sixteen centuries ago that liberty exists in being able to choose that which is ultimately good.[65] It is not a selection between competing goods but, in every situation, the selection of that which alone is good. Only three things can keep us from choosing the good, namely, ignorance, internal compulsion, and external coercion. Where these exist, we are acting not in freedom, but under restriction. The human person always chooses that which he or she perceives to be personally good at the immediate moment when the choice is made. The fact that our choice turns out not to be good, or that, in the end, it does not bring lasting happiness, is often due to the fact that we did not perceive it as it truly was. We were mistaken. We acted out of ignorance. We were not free.

At other times, we may feel overcome by an internal compulsion to choose as good that which is not good at all; yet, at the moment, it seemed like it was good for us. We never choose evil because we think it will be bad for us. Rather, we choose evil because right then, when the choice is made, it seems like something that for us will be good. In retrospect, an individual often says, I chose what was evil because at that moment I thought that it was good for me. Unless we are free from compulsion we cannot experience true liberty. Finally, we may choose only an apparent good because factors or persons or events outside our own selves constrain us to make wrong choices. We are influenced to choose a lesser good, or something that is not good at all.

At the moment we are not concerned with the question of moral culpability; in determining that, there are other factors to be considered. This is a question of how the human psyche operates. Our very nature disposes us to choose what we perceive to be *good for us*. Were we totally liberated from selfishness and self-centeredness, from ignorance of the truth, from compulsions of the heart, and from outside influences, then we would be truly free. Under the influence of sin, the human condition is the experience of ignorance, compulsion, and coercion. Under sin, the best that we can hope for is the illusion of freedom when we experience the power of choice. That's why so many people confuse freedom of choice with real freedom. It is only when we are under the influence of grace, as St. Augustine knew, that we experience true liberty, for only under grace can we be freed from ignorance, from the compulsions of the heart, and from the power of outside influence.[66] Without true freedom, making the right choice is largely a matter of luck, and choosing for God may well nigh be impossible. Since we can receive only what we are disposed to receive, freedom is a necessary disposition for one who would choose rightly.

Reception of the Eucharist

Often people are heard to remark that despite frequent attendance at Mass and Communion, they do not find themselves to be better persons or feel closer to God. Shouldn't receiving Communion make a real difference in our lives right now? Shouldn't grace make a difference in the way we live? Shouldn't we find ourselves drawn closer and closer to God? Perhaps the issue is not with the Eucharist itself, but with the manner in which we receive it. Not only knowledge and faith, but also advertence are necessary dispositions for the reception of the sacraments. Without advertence we do not receive the fullness of grace, the full benefit of the Eucharist.

St. Thomas Aquinas recognized the importance of knowledge and faith in the reception of the Eucharist. He speaks, for instance, of the mouse that consumes a portion of the Eucharist left exposed. Does the mouse receive the body of Christ, Aquinas asks, or does it merely eat the accidents through which the body of Christ is made present? Aquinas answers that the mouse cannot receive the Eucharist since it lacks knowledge of the Eucharist, even though Christ remains present there under the accidents that are apparent to the senses.[67] He goes even a step further by affirming that a believer who consumes the consecrated bread thinking that it is not consecrated does not receive the Eucharist or the grace of the sacrament because this person is unaware of Christ's real presence. This individual receives only the accidents of bread, although Christ is truly present there.

To go a step further still, what of those who know that others believe the Eucharist to be the real presence of Christ but who, themselves, do not believe it? A person may decide, nonetheless, to take Communion along with others at the Mass, even though this individual has no personal faith in the Eucharist at all. Do non-believers receive the body of Christ in the Eucharist that they consume? Again, Aquinas responds in the negative, since such individuals do not, themselves, believe, despite their knowledge of the faith of others. They consume the accidents through which Christ is offered, but they do not receive the substance which is offered. They have no contact with the reality of Christ present in the Eucharist. They receive the Eucharist, "not as sacrament, but as simple food."

This brings us to a final question. What of believers who know with the knowledge of faith that Christ is present in the Eucharist, who, in fact, believe in Christ's presence with true internal conviction, but who, on a particular occasion, receive the Eucharist in a state of distraction and with no immediate attention to what is taking place? With our minds focused everywhere but on the Eucharist, with our attention drawn to crying children, to the overcrowded parking lot we hope quickly to escape, or to the televised football game we are missing at the moment, we may fail to give real advertence to the Eucharistic presence of Christ, even as we consume it. Do we, in fact, receive the body of Christ? Do we receive the grace of the sacrament? At the very least, we cannot be said to receive the fullness of grace which the sacrament offers, for we can only fully receive what we are fully disposed to receive.

When approaching the Eucharist, if we expect to receive the grace which the sacrament has to offer, we must do so not only with knowledge and faith, but also with full advertence, that is, with prayerful attention, reverent devotion, and a practical commitment to living our faith in action. When such advertence is consciously attained, we may well expect to sense the presence of Christ in our lives and to find that the Eucharist does change how we live. Where divine gifts are involved — gifts of revelation, grace, and sacrament — knowledge, faith, and advertence dispose our minds and our hearts to receive them.

Chapter 4

"Scriptural Interpretation
Is a Work of the Whole Church"

Nearly twenty-five years ago, while in my first assignment as a parish priest, I found myself one noontime seated next to an evangelical pastor at a local ecumenical luncheon. After some time, the conversation turned to the question of the correct interpretation of Scripture. We both agreed that among the readership of the Bible there exist innumerable interpretations of individual passages of Scripture and that these interpretations are often irreconcilable with one another. We discussed how any given passage was to be correctly understood. While I emphasized the importance of biblical criticism and the necessity of authority and Tradition in the interpretation of Scripture, he flatly disagreed. These, he said, are merely tools for literary study, historical research, and the governance of a hierarchical institution, such as the Catholic Church. They are unnecessary for the person who lives by faith. Rather, he claimed, the Holy Spirit individually inspires the authentic believer in the correct interpretation of any given passage.

It is possible, he continued, that God may communicate a message for one believer that differs from that which God communicates to another, as long as the messages are not at total variance. Where irreconcilable interpretations do exist, he claimed, it is only necessary to distinguish the authentic believer from one whose faith has been corrupted by false values or personal interests. If the Bible is truly an inspired book, he persisted, it must be possible for readers in every age to understand the truth of the message according to the modes of thinking and writing characteristic of their own times. Study of the past may enhance their appreciation for God's word in Scripture, but is not necessary for living a life inspired by the Holy Spirit today. After all, he concluded, without personal inspiration, no reader could recognize the true message of the Bible. An inspired text demands an inspired reader.

I disagree with much of what my evangelical associate said on that occasion, but I have to agree with his final statement: an inspired text does require an inspired reader. Still, who is the inspired reader of Scripture and how is that inspired reader to be identified? How can an individual be certain that his or her own understanding of Scripture is inspired by God and that the interpretation arrived at is correct? Is it possible that God can communicate a personal message to an individual reader that is not communicated to other readers of the same text, and that this personal communication is both inspired and true? Is an inspired work really freed from the ordinary processes of literary criticism; can the text stand alone in time, liberated from the period in which it was composed, so that readers in every age can understand the truth of the message according to the modes of thinking and writing characteristic of their own times and without any recourse to the past? Finally, is an inspired reader actually dispensed from the necessity of biblical study, requiring only biblical reflection for a correct interpretation and application of Scripture? Many faithful Christians, both within and outside the Catholic Church, appear to answer the latter questions in the affirmative, but are they correct?

Today, one can read the Bible as a work of literature or as a work of faith. Either way, it must be interpreted to be correctly understood — as literature, according to the principles of literary criticism; as a faith document, according to the principles of belief. Literary criticism is not concerned with the question of divine inspiration. It looks no further than the written text itself and the impression which the text makes upon the reader. Whether God utilizes the written word to communicate God's presence and revelation to humankind is not the interest or focus of the literary critic. Rather, literary criticism attempts to discover what individuals, whether believers or non-believers, would consider the most authentic meaning of a written work by carefully examining all the literary devices employed by the writer, the environment and circumstances in which the work was written, the audiences originally and subsequently addressed, and the author's conscious and unconscious motivations. The poetic or literary inspiration of the writer, considered in purely human terms, is the literary critic's concern; divine inspiration is not. Admiration for the style and accomplishment of the author is a desirable consideration for the student of literature; the engendering of religious faith in the reader very often is not.

Many factors influence the poetic or literary inspiration of a writer, including religious faith, and the author cannot be aware of them all. Consequently, a writer may often say more than he or she consciously intends. Arriving at the fuller understanding of what was written is a legitimate goal for the literary critic, who may give consideration to religious as well as secular influences on the author and the author's accomplishments. Readers of a different place and time, encountering a work of literature in entirely different circumstances than those of the author, may discover new meanings about which the author had no awareness. If these meanings are true to the text itself, they may unveil authentic insights for the reader and the literary critic. It is safe to say, however, that literary criticism need not concern itself with religious faith, and the reader or critic who approaches the biblical text in this manner need not be a believer to appreciate the literary accomplishment which the Bible represents. As a result, many courses on the Bible as literature are taught in public schools and universities without raising legal concerns about the separation of Church and State. Studying the Bible within the context of faith, however, is an entirely different matter.

The Bible was written in faith for people who believe. It was written to express the faith convictions of a believing community, and it was written to bring others into that same community of faith. It is important to remember that both the Old and New Testaments were written over a lengthy period of time and only after the Jewish nation and the Christian Church had lived out their faith for a number of years. It was not the Scriptures which formed the faith of these communities. Rather, it was the faith of these communities which formed the Scriptures. If the Scriptures are inspired, it is because the communities which composed them were inspired. If the Scriptures are to be understood as inspired not only in the process of their composition, but for today's readers as well, this must be because they are interpreted by communities and individuals who read them under inspiration. Knowing the faith of the first communities and the transmission of that faith through the centuries is a vital component in the process of inspired interpretation. As the Fathers of the Second Vatican Council noted, "Sacred Scripture must be read and interpreted in the light of the same Spirit by whom it was written" (*Dei Verbum*, 12).

Divine inspiration, however, does not bypass the normal processes of human authorship. The same processes of literary interpretation that assist in the understanding of any literary work have a part to play in determining the meaning of an inspired text. Inspired interpretation takes into account the motivation and intention of the human authors, the literary devices which they employed, the audiences for whom they wrote and the readers who subsequently received their texts, the environment and circumstances in which they wrote, and all the factors that played upon their subconscious minds and served to influence the final composition. In addition, inspired interpretation gives proper weight to the influence of grace and the activity of God working upon the conscious and subconscious minds of the human authors. As the Fathers of the Second Vatican Council carefully stated, "Since God speaks in Sacred Scripture through men in human fashion, the interpreter of Sacred Scripture, in order to see clearly what God wanted to communicate to us, should carefully investigate what meaning the sacred writers really intended, and what God wanted to manifest by means of their words." Moreover, "the interpreter must investigate what meaning the sacred writer intended to express and actually expressed in particular circumstances as he used contemporary literary forms in accordance with the situation of his own time and culture." Finally, "the living tradition of the whole Church must be taken into account" since to the judgment of the Church has been entrusted the "divine commission and ministry of guarding and interpreting the word of God" (*Dei Verbum,* 12). Nonetheless, even with a proper use of literary criticism, only a reader who has been inspired in his interpretation can arrive at the authentic meaning of an inspired text. An inspired text does require an inspired reader.

Like the Old Testament, the New Testament was composed in stages over time. Jesus himself was not known to have written down any of his teachings. Rather, he busied himself with proclaiming orally the word of his Father, expressing himself according to the style of his own time. According to the normal process of human understanding, his hearers absorbed what he said, comprehending his words according to their own abilities and experience. They, in turn, passed on his teaching to their disciples and listeners, doing so partly in writing, but to a much greater extent in their own oral teaching and preaching. In light of the resurrection event, they acquired a fuller understanding of the meaning of Jesus' words and deeds, and they sought to communicate that meaning according to the forms of literary and oral communication characteristic of their age. Eventually they and others committed to writing the fundamental teachings of Jesus along with the fuller understanding acquired by the disciples and evangelists. Through a process of selection, synthesis, and explication, the written text was edited to express the particular purpose of the writer and to appeal to the understanding and faith of those for whom he wrote.[68]

The evangelists and writers of the New Testament made use of history and allegory, prophecy and poetry, analogy and other forms of literary expression to convey not merely the data of Jesus' life and teaching, but, more importantly, the meaning of his life and the significance of his message. Where they did engage in historical writing, it was not as we commonly understand history to be written today; it was not a journalistic account of people, places, dates, and events, all following in strictly chronological order. Rather, they selected their details and shaped their accounts, conveying the truth of their teaching through language that is sometimes figurative and often analogical. The author of the Gospel of John is very explicit about his method and his intention: "Jesus performed many other signs as well — signs not recorded here — in the presence of his disciples. But these have been recorded to help you believe that Jesus is the Messiah, the Son of God, so that through this faith you may have life in his name" (John 20:30–31). A chapter later he concludes, "It is this same disciple [the 'beloved disciple'] who is the witness to these things; it is he who wrote them down and his testimony, we know, is true. There are still many other things that Jesus did, yet if they were written about in detail, I doubt there would be room enough in the entire world to hold the books to record them" (John 21:24–25).

The evangelist admits to having made a selection of events for the explicit purpose of leading his readers to faith. The Johannine scribe, like the other writers of the New Testament, wrote his text from within a community of believers who were well aware of the truth of his teaching, for their believing had preceded his writing. The inspired text grew from the inspired community. Similarly, it would take a reader inspired by grace to rightly comprehend the truth of what was written. An inspired text requires an inspired reader, but the inspired reader must be in touch with the inspired community. In fact, since the inspired text was written from within the inspired community, expressing the faith of that community, and to benefit the community's own members — present and future — the proper interpreter of the text is the community itself, a community secure in the faith handed down to it from the apostles. It was with this in mind that St. Paul wrote to the Church at Galatia, lamenting that some members were abandoning the faith of the community in their search for personal revelation.

> I am amazed that you are so soon deserting him who called you in accord with his gracious design in Christ, and are going over to another gospel. But there is no other. Some who wish to alter the gospel of Christ must have confused you. For even if we, or an angel from heaven, should preach to you a gospel not in accord with the one we delivered to you, let a curse be upon him! I repeat what I have just said: if anyone preaches a gospel to you other than the one you received, let a curse be upon him. (Gal 1:6–8)

The author of the Second Letter of Peter likewise warns his readers against the rise of false prophets and false teachers who come proclaiming personal interpretations at variance with the faith of the entire community. "First you must understand this," he writes. "There is no prophecy contained in Scripture which is a personal interpretation. Prophecy has never been put forward by man's willing it. It is rather that men impelled by the Holy Spirit have spoken under God's influence" (2 Pet 1:20–21). The author warns his readers to hold fast to the teachings of the apostles that have been handed down to the entire Church and to interpret the message of Scripture according to the faith they received from those who were "altogether reliable," from the apostles who heard the message "from heaven" itself. The Scriptures were written from the position of faith as that faith was received, understood and passed on by the first Christian communi-

ties. Therefore, it is within that same community of faith,
in every place where it is to be found, that the Scriptures
continue to be received, understood, and transmitted. Outside the community of faith there is no guarantee that the
Scriptures will be properly interpreted and understood. An
inspired text demands an inspired reader and *the* inspired
reader of Scripture is the whole community of the Church
itself.

Early on, the Fathers of the Church understood this basic
truth of scriptural interpretation. In the third century, Origen
testified that there are many who feel themselves qualified to
interpret Scripture, but only those who are members of the
community and one with the entire Church in its apostolic
tradition can be truly understood to be inspired.[69] Tertullian, a generation before, professed that wherever the truth
of Christian discipline and faith are clearly present, there also
will be found the truth of the Scriptures and their proper
interpretation.[70] Earlier still, in the second century, St. Irenaeus claimed that the Church alone properly interprets the
Scriptures since divine inspiration is accorded to the Church
through the succession of bishops.[71] St. Augustine likewise
taught that the unanimity of the bishops with the Fathers
of the Church who preceded them assures the continuation
of inspired interpretation.[72] Echoing this same doctrine, Vincent of Lerins, writing in the fifth century, offered his famous
dictum that only those teachings are to be accepted as true
which have been commonly received, held, and handed on
through time. Even if a holy man holds something to be
true, he continued, it is only to be accepted as personal opinion if not commonly held, no matter how saintly the person
may be.[73] There are so many interpretations of Scripture,
he concluded, that the most authentic must be that which

is in accord with the standard of ecclesiastical and universal meaning.[74]

Not only was the composition of the individual books of Scripture an exercise of divine inspiration, so also was the establishment of the canon of Scripture — the process of identifying and compiling into one Bible all the individual scriptural texts officially and universally recognized by the Church. The Spirit that inspired the writing of Scripture, and that continues to inspire its correct interpretation, is the same Spirit that directed the Church to discern the canon of Scripture. Statements from the Muratorian Fragment, reflecting the teaching of the second half of the second century, support the conclusion that only those books could be entered into Scripture and read publicly in the assembly of the faithful which the Church as a whole had been moved by the Holy Spirit to recognize as inspired.[75]

Originally, the books of the New Testament were circulated individually within and among the various Christian communities. Testimonies of Jesus' mission and teaching, letters written by apostles and evangelizers, historical accounts of the growth of the Church and the exploits of the apostles, and commentaries on living the Christian life in the face of present and future conflict were read aloud at liturgical services and gatherings of the faithful. Some of these works found acceptance in only a limited number of communities and were eventually eliminated from canons or lists of official texts. Others that at first found only limited acceptance, eventually were adopted by communities everywhere. It took several centuries before an official listing was compiled, and centuries more before the Church formally declared that no other texts could be added to the Bible.[76]

The process of compiling a universally recognized canon

of Scripture was not one of official selection by the hierar-
chy of the Church. Rather, it was a process of communal
discernment by all the churches in union with one another.
Voicing the general doctrine of the Church Fathers, St. Cyril
of Jerusalem stated that it was through the inspiration of the
Holy Spirit that the Scriptures were written and that it was
through the same divine inspiration that the Church recognized those Scriptures as true and caused them to be read
aloud within the liturgy itself. Only those which the Church
accepted as true and permitted to be read in the liturgy,
he concluded, could be considered inspired.[77] The fourth-
century Council of Laodicea set this same doctrine into law
when it declared that only those books are canonical which
the Church has been inspired to recognize as properly belonging to the canon of Scripture. These alone are to be read
publicly in the Church.[78]

St. Augustine emphasized the continuity of recognition
through the centuries when he wrote that only those books
can be known as authentic which have been received by
the whole Church, or by the most eminent churches, continuing through the succession of bishops from the time of
the apostles to our own day.[79] Universal acceptance by the
whole Church, widespread use within the liturgy, and general recognition by communities with apostolic succession
became the norms for recognizing scriptural texts as being
inspired and worthy of canonicity. Finally, when the Gospel
of Luke was called into question because of its association
with the heresy of Marcion, Tertullian defended its continued
acceptance on the basis that it had always been recognized by
the whole Church as inspired.[80] Without an inspired reader,
an inspired book would remain unrecognized. Without an
inspired interpreter, an inspired work would be largely inef-

fective. An inspired text demands an inspired reader, and *the* inspired reader of Scripture is the whole Church itself.

Related Doctrines

Related to this notion of biblical inspiration are other key doctrines of the Church, namely, revelation, biblical inerrancy, and the place of the Scriptures in the Church. Each of these doctrines is based on the understanding that God can and does inspire knowledge of the truth. Inspired by divine grace, the Church is capable of comprehending with certainty more than what the individual human intellect, left to itself, could ever expect to acquire.

Revelation

While inspiration is concerned with the medium of God's self-communication, revelation concerns the nature and content of what God has chosen to communicate. Revelation does not ultimately concern itself with what the human intellect is capable of discerning through experience, observation, and reason alone. Rather, revelation exceeds native human intelligence by making known through divine assistance those things which can be known in no other way. This concerns, first of all, God's own self and what God chooses to make known to us about Godself. Through human reasoning, we can surmise that God exists and that God is the origin of the creation that surrounds us. From observation of the world, we may even abstract certain qualities and apply them to God. Unity, goodness, truth, and beauty were significant values in Greek philosophy, but how can we know for certain that the divine is not also multiple, dualistic, inconstant, and disordered? The study of religious anthropology reveals systems of belief that have attributed to God, or the gods, these very qualities. The history of philosophy instructs us that unaided reason can, with certainty, conceive nothing more substantial about God than a remote principle of being and origin of all that exists. Philosophy alone cannot assure us of a God who is personal, intimate, and responsive to our human needs. Certainly, we often experience innate longings for transcendence, attractions to ethical principles and noble ideals, and a sense of being in the presence of something or someone greater than ourselves, but without revelation we cannot know for certain that this experience is an awareness of God. It is precisely revelation that assures us that God is real and that God is personal, intimate, and concerned about us.

Many people understand revelation in propositional terms, that is, as a list of doctrines, instructions, and statements to be accepted on faith. However, revelation is not simply the transmission of information formerly hidden from human reason and now expressed in sentences and propositions. Revelation is, in fact, primarily the communication of the mystery of God to us and only secondarily the unfolding of propositions about God, about the divine presence in creation and history, and about our own final end. Within a Christian context the opening verses of the Letter to the Hebrews expresses best of all the nature of revelation. "In times past, God spoke in fragmentary and varied ways to our fathers through the prophets; in this, the final age, he has spoken to us through his Son, whom he made heir of all things and through whom he first created the universe" (Heb 1:1–2).

While we may concede elements of truth and even of revelation among the many religions of the world, for us as Christians, revelation is above all the person of Jesus himself, Jesus who is "the reflection of the Father's glory, the exact representation of the Father's being," who "sustains all things by his powerful word," and who "has taken his seat at the right hand of the Majesty in heaven, as far superior to the angels as the name he has inherited is superior to theirs" (Heb 1:3–4). Everything we have come to believe as Christians is based on this one profound truth, that Jesus is the wisdom and the power of God and that all he has told us is true. This revelation is made available to all who believe. Its very significance rests in the fact that it has not been made known to only a few, but that it has been the constant understanding of an entire community of believers from the first century until today. It has not been given for the salvation of each individual alone, but for the salvation of all people and of the entire world (Tit 2:11).

Many people search for personal revelation, for the knowledge of something hidden from others but made known to them alone. The very basis of gnostic belief in all its manifestations throughout history is the conviction that some can be given knowledge of supernatural truths that remain hidden from all but the elect. The very appeal of many new age spiritualities is to be among the chosen to whom arcane knowledge is revealed. I do not deny that God can make known to individuals particular insights that may pertain to them alone, or that may have significance for a particular community of individuals or for the Church in a given time or place; nevertheless, the revelation that pertains to salvation is a revelation that is given for all. Its significance is that it is public revelation intended for everyone, not private revelation meant for a few. Unless it is recognized by the whole community of believers, unless it is consistent with the faith handed down from the apostles, unless it is the constant belief of the Church through the centuries, then it cannot be the revelation proclaimed in Scripture for the salvation of the whole world.

The reliability of revealed truth is that the entire community of faith, at all times and in all places, recognizes it as true. Individuals may be deceived; history is filled with the stories of deluded individuals whose private revelations turned out to be violent and false. Entire communities may be deceived; religious cults based on private revelations often turn destructive and self-annihilating. The only private revelation that can be relied upon is that which is consistent with the public revelation made available to all. God's truth cannot contradict itself. The revelation given to some cannot contradict the revelation given to all. If an inspired text demands an inspired reader, then the truth of revelation requires a recipient who has been given the grace to recognize the truth. If the only certainly inspired interpreter of Scripture is the whole Church itself, then the only certain revelation is that which the whole Church recognizes and calls its own.

Biblical Inerrancy

Some readers of the Bible are quick to label its entire teaching as unreliable because of factual inaccuracies and the evidence of discredited scientific theories. The four Gospels themselves disagree about the chronology of certain events in the life of Jesus, the exact wording of many of his statements, and conflicting details in the narrative accounts. In the wake of the nineteenth-century attempt to construct scientific history, the Bible has been subjected to standards inconsistent with the time frame in which the Scriptures were written. In the interest of upholding the truth of the Bible, some writers have attempted to rationalize discrepancies by fabricating implausible explanations. To take a single example, did Jesus ascend to heaven from a mountaintop in Galilee, as Matthew's Gospel recounts (28:16–20), or from a spot near Bethany in Judea, as Luke's Gospel records (24:50–52); or did he enact the Ascension on two separate occasions for different groups of disciples, as some literal interpreters of the Bible have expounded? Is it even necessary to reconcile these two differing accounts, both of which testify to the reality of the Ascension? Might it not be enough to note a common belief in the significance of Jesus' departure from this world and his return to the right hand of the Father? In reality, the Gospel writers were far more concerned with the meaning of Jesus' life than with the exact details of his life story. It is precisely in this context that the inerrancy of Scripture is to be understood.

The Gospel writers were not interested in presenting a detailed journalistic accounting of the life of Jesus, a biography in the contemporary understanding of the genre. They do not record historical data for the sheer accumulation of facts. Rather, the Gospels are a combination of factual memories and religious insights, faithful to the memory of Jesus but creative in expressing the meaning of his life and in shaping the narrative in which that meaning is conveyed. The Gospels are, in effect, joined fragments, each with its own purpose and particular theological approach. At the core of each Gospel is the early Church kerygma about the crucified-and-risen Lord. This core is surrounded by other aspects of each evangelist's theological insight. The concern of the early Church was the presence of Jesus in their midst, the message of his words and the meaning of his actions. They were not overly concerned about the accuracy of their details as long as the meaning of his life and the message of his teaching were correctly conveyed. It is a twentieth-century preoccupation to be concerned about the exact citation of every statement and action, as if the least deviation could call into question the validity of what is recorded. The evangelists, on the other hand, seemed to freely develop and alter historical circumstances, to pick and choose the events they wanted to relate, even to change the context or the sequence of events if this would more clearly express their theological intent and the truth they wanted to convey.

Not only the Gospels but the whole of the Old and New Testaments need to be interpreted according to the standards of composition particular to their own time. The truth of the Scriptures is to be found in carefully investigating "what meaning the sacred writers intended and what God wanted to manifest by means of their words"(*Dei Verbum,* 12). It is with this in mind that the Fathers of the Second Vatican Council stated that "the books of Scripture must be acknowledged as teaching firmly, faithfully, and without error that truth which God wanted put into the sacred writings for the sake of our salvation" (*Dei Verbum,* 11). Not every detail contained in the Bible needs to be accurately related for the message of the Scriptures to be conveyed without error.

What guarantees inerrancy and the recognition of biblical truth is the active presence of the Holy Spirit within the community of the Church. As Catholics, we are "people of the book," but we are also "people of the Tradition." We stand in the midst of a living Tradition, confident that the words of Jesus in the Gospel of John will continue to be ful-filled: "The Paraclete, the Holy Spirit whom the Father will send in my name, will instruct you in everything, and remind you of all that I told you" (John 14:26). "When he comes, however, being the Spirit of truth, he will guide you to all truth" (John 16:13). In the fourth century, St. Epiphanius of Salamis wrote that the Tradition of the Church is as in-spired as the Scriptures themselves.[81] Standing in this living Tradition, the Church as a whole is the inspired interpreter of Scripture, not just the Church of the first century, when the Gospels were composed, and not just the Church of today, engaged in a dynamic process of biblical study and scriptural interpretation. The Church as a whole includes the Church throughout the ages. Knowing how the Church in the past understood and interpreted the Bible will protect us from misinterpreting the word of God today. Biblical inerrancy is dependent upon the active presence of the Holy Spirit in both the composition and the interpretation of Scripture. An inspired text requires an inspired reader, and the inspired reader of Scripture is the whole Church itself.

The Place of the Scriptures in the Church

The ministry of the Church is a ministry of word and sacra-ment. Thus the Church proclaims the liturgy of the Eucharist to be the source and summit of its entire life since, in the celebration of the liturgy, the equal primacy of word and sacrament is made clearly apparent.[82] In this regard the Fa-thers of the Second Vatican Council stated, "The Church has always venerated the divine Scriptures just as she ven-erates the body of the Lord, since from the table of both the word of God and of the body of Christ she unceasingly re-

ceives and offers to the faithful the bread of life, especially in
the sacred liturgy" (*Dei Verbum,* 21). The Church, however,
does not view itself exclusively as a "people of the book"
for whom the Sacred Scriptures constitute the sole rule of
faith. The lived reality of faith preceded the submission of
that faith to writing and the compilation of the Bible. Rather,
the Church considers the Scriptures to be a distinctive and
definitive element within the sacred Tradition that has been
handed down from generation to generation and that continues to find an ever fuller expression in the life of the faithful.
Thus, in the words of the Council Fathers, "Sacred tradition
and Sacred Scripture form one sacred deposit of the word
of God, which is committed to the Church." In turn, the
Church "has always regarded the Scriptures together with
sacred tradition as the supreme rule of faith, and ever will
do so" (*Dei Verbum,* 10 and 21).

The Scriptures serve an essential function within the living
Tradition of the Church. Capturing the faith of the apostolic
age to which the Christian community in every succeed-
ing era must be faithful, Scripture provides a standard of
judgment for later Church teaching and practice. While doctrines may continue to develop in clarity of understanding
through the process of theological investigation, and those
which were lesser known in a previous age may become more
clearly understood and defined with the passage of time,
such teaching must always be consistent with the faith of
the early Church as that faith has been set down for us in
Scripture and the apostolic witness. In this sense Scripture
stands above and interprets the community of the Church today. At the same time, the Church is the steward of the Bible
and understands and explains it in the light of the consistent
faith and practice of the Christian community throughout

the centuries. Thus, the Church stands in a dialectical relationship with the Scriptures and interprets them for today. Together, Scripture and Tradition constitute a hermeneutical circle within which the Scriptures interpret the faith of the Church and the Church interprets the meaning of the Scriptures. This hermeneutical circle begs answers to two questions: Is the community of today faithful to Scripture? Is Scripture understood according to the lived experience of the faith community as it continues to move through time and history?

The Holy Spirit, the primary author of Scripture, is also the Paraclete who guides the Church in all understanding. The Spirit who inspired the writing of Scripture is the same Spirit who inspires the Church to correctly comprehend and interpret the word of God set down in writing and continuously experienced in the life of the community. The word of God continues to challenge the Church whenever the Scriptures are read and proclaimed. At the same time, in the act of proclaiming the Scriptures, the Church is not simply passing on a dead manuscript from the past, but the living word of God manifest in the living Tradition and faith of the people. An inspired text demands an inspired reader, and the inspired reader of Scripture is the whole Church animated by the presence of the Holy Spirit.

Implications for an Applied Theology

At the outset of this chapter, questions about the personal interpretation of Scripture were raised and still remain to be answered. In the broader context, this is an inquiry into private revelation: does God use Scripture and other means of disclosure to communicate private revelations to individual persons? In the narrower context, this is an issue of methodology: how does anyone, setting out to read the Bible for oneself, develop a sense of confidence that he or she is correctly understanding and interpreting the word of God? From the theological notion of inspiration several significant implications arise, among them, the validity of private revelation and the reliability of personal biblical interpretation.

Private Revelation

There are not a few people who, when faced with important decisions, consult the Bible by opening its pages at random and selecting the first passage on which their eyes focus. In the life story of St. Francis of Assisi it is recorded that this was the method he used in discerning God's will for him. Confused about the future direction of his life, it is said, he opened the Bible and randomly selected the passage in Matthew's Gospel about the rich young man: "If you seek perfection, go, sell your possessions and give to the poor. You will then have treasure in heaven. Afterward, come back and follow me" (Matt 19:21). Whether Francis actually arrived at his decision in this manner is really unimportant. What is momentous is the fact that he understood this passage as a private revelation intended for himself personally, and his response to that revelation changed not only his life but the life of the entire Church.

God can inspire us personally through our reading of Scripture. In any given instance, a receptive reader may be inspired by the Holy Spirit to understand a passage of Scripture in a manner that has particular application to his or her own life, or to the lives of others, to an entire community or even to the whole Church at a particular time in history. Still the question remains, how can a single individual be certain that God has inspired in the reader a revelation of particular significance for that individual's life and for the lives of others? Sometimes we may be mistaken. On another occasion, for example, after a period of meditation and prayer over various passages of Scripture, St. Francis sensed that the figure of Christ on the crucifix before which he was praying spoke to him, instructing him to rebuild the church. For a time he occupied himself in repairing the ruined church of San Damiano in Assisi. It was only later that Francis realized it was the entire Church that God was calling him to repair.

Often, time is the measure of genuine revelation. It was only after the resurrection that Jesus' disciples realized that he himself was the final public revelation of the Father given to all people. It was only with the passage of time that the success of his mendicant brothers proved the truth of the private revelation given to Francis. The immediate indication of a true private revelation, however, is its continuity and correspondence with the public revelation given to all, with the revelation proclaimed as doctrine by the Church. The Holy Spirit is the author of revelation and would not contradict the revelation definitively preserved by the Church. An indispensable sign of validity is the compatibility of private revelation with the understanding of faith held by the universal faith community. No matter how convinced we may be that God has spoken a message for us alone, we must be willing to measure the content of that message against the fuller understanding of faith consistently communicated to us by the Church down through the centuries. Individually,

God may inspire our reading of Scripture, but the certainly inspired reader of Scripture is the Church itself.

Personal Interpretation

In his argument with the Manichaean propagandist Faustus of Milevis, St. Augustine wrote, "It is possible for even a faithful reader to misunderstand the meaning of the Scriptures."[83] Personal interpretation is not an automatic process, even for one who has been inspired by the Holy Spirit. Every passage must be read in the context in which it was written and compared with the entire body of Sacred Scripture. Out of context, an individual passage may be easily distorted and falsely interpreted. Of course, the more a person reads the Bible and becomes familiar with its content, the greater facility of interpretation he or she achieves. No biblical text stands alone in time, liberated from the period in which it was composed or from the process by which its meaning has been transmitted through the centuries. Readers of a later age cannot with certainty understand the truth of what was written simply by applying the modes of thinking and writing characteristic of their own later time. Even an inspired reader is not excused from the necessity of careful biblical study.

In ascertaining the truth of a particular passage, the Church itself makes use of expert biblical scholars who are adept both at textual criticism and at historical analysis. If the entire faith community is the inspired interpreter of Scripture, then the Church of today must not content itself with simply knowing its own mind. It must also know the mind of the apostolic community that first wrote the Scriptures, as well as the mind of each successive faith community that transmitted through the centuries their understanding of those Scriptures. Even the Holy Father relies on the work of his Pontifical Biblical Commission in providing the expertise which the Church requires as one essential component of faithful interpretation. In the same way, the individual reader of Scripture should avoid the arrogance of assuming that he or she can dispense with the assistance of biblical experts.

The individual reader, like the Church itself, needs to ask several indispensable questions of any biblical passage in order to understand it with assurance. Recourse to the work of biblical scholars will also be indispensable in answering these questions. What did it mean for those who first heard the spoken word of God or experienced God's activity in their midst? What did it mean for those who wrote it down? Why did they write this passage and not another, and why did they write it in precisely this way and not in another? What did it mean for those who preserved it and passed it on? Finally, what does it mean for us today? In answering these questions we come face to face with the various stages of biblical composition and the transmission of the text.[84]

At the first stage, we seek to understand the original deeds of God in the history of Israel, the words of Israel's prophets and teachers, and, in particular, the words and deeds of Jesus, all expressed according to the style of their times. What did the people of those times hear and experience, and what did they think about it? Historical criticism is the tool for discerning the content of this stage of the Tradition. The second stage is concerned with the oral transmission of the message in the light of the fuller understanding accorded by time. This is particularly true of the composition of the New Testament, which begins with the preaching of the first disciples after the resurrection and Pentecost events. They expressed their fuller understanding of Jesus through different forms of communication, for example, catechesis, narratives, testimonies, hymns, prayers, and doxologies. Form criticism is the indispensable tool for understanding this stage of the Tradition. In the third stage, when the text was edited and set into writing, the writer shaped the text through a process of selection, synthesis, and explication in order to express a particular purpose or dominant theme. Redaction criticism is the tool that helps us to understand the dominant ideas that determined the final edition of the written text.

The various communities of faith that read, preserved, and transmitted the sacred text played several significant roles in the next stage of the Tradition. They discerned what is authentic Scripture and what is not, preserving the former and setting aside the latter. Beyond that, these communities preserved commentary on the word of God, expressing through letters, sermons, theological disputations, doctrinal explications, and moral exhortations the very truths which they found the Scriptures to reveal. The recorded history of their times tells us how they understood the Scriptures and made use of them in defending and living the faith that had been transmitted to them. Finally, in our own day, Sacred Scripture continues to be at the core of Christian experience, even as that experience incorporates itself into the lives and cultures of an increasingly diverse Church. Knowing how the Christian faith is lived today and how the Scriptures are understood in the context of every living expression of faith is also essential for biblical interpretation.

We stand in a living Tradition that incorporates both past and present in a dynamic process of scriptural interpretation. We need to know the faith of the community, the community existing through the centuries, the community existing today. We cannot avoid the question, how has the Church always understood the word of God and each passage of Scripture? An inspired text requires an inspired reader. The whole Church, in every age, is the inspired reader and interpreter of Scripture. We need the humility to accept this truth, even as we search out and seek to interpret the full meaning of the Scriptures for ourselves. Not everyone who opens the Bible is capable of interpreting it correctly.

Chapter 5

"Great Ideas Develop over Time"

Of the theologians of the nineteenth century, John Henry Newman remains a major influence on theology today. Newman was first ordained to priesthood as an Anglican in 1825 and twenty-two years later in the Roman Catholic Church. In 1879 he was named a cardinal by Pope Leo XIII, but only after considerable controversy had come to surround Dr. Newman and his writings. Pope Leo used the cardinalate as a way of sanctioning Newman's theology without alienating his opponents. Nearly a century later, the theology of Cardinal Newman would have considerable influence on the teachings of the Second Vatican Council, but not until it had weathered the Modernist crisis.

For Newman, the process of his conversion from Anglicanism to Roman Catholicism was a matter of lengthy and thorough theological study and agonized soul searching. Most of what Catholicism taught about Scripture, sacraments, and salvation Newman already professed in the Anglican Church. There he also found his prayer life well nourished, his search for holiness encouraged, and his pastoral labors rewarded. At the same time, many of the trappings of Catholicism disturbed him, particularly the place held by the saints and the Blessed Virgin in Catholic devotionalism and the exaggerated sentimentalism of many of its religious customs and ceremonies as he experienced them. Moreover, becoming a Catholic in nineteenth-century England carried serious consequences, especially for one who had already become a well-known scholar and preacher at Oxford. The greatest difficulty for Newman, however, was the number of doctrines professed by Catholics that did not appear well established in Scripture and that seemed to be accretions to the revealed truths handed down from the apostolic period. Anglicans were convinced that the Church of Rome, despite its antiquity and claims to apostolic succession, had tampered with the deposit of faith handed down from the apostles.

Newman set for himself a course of study. He thoroughly researched these late Catholic doctrines and gradually became convinced that they were legitimate developments. He concluded that sufficient traces of these doctrines existed in the early Church to justify their fuller expression in a later age. On the assumption that divine providence was continuing to guide the Church throughout history, the "Roman additions" could be explained as a fuller realization of the deposit of faith. In 1844 Newman decided to work out his theory on the development of doctrine in a formal treatise on the topic. Within a year he was convinced that the Roman doctrines were correct, and he no longer felt at home in the Anglican Church. He would have to seek reception into the Church of Rome. This he did on October 9, 1845. Four months later, in February of the following year, he left his beloved Oxford University and his parish home at Littlemore and in September departed for Rome.

The treatise he had begun as an Anglican, *An Essay on the Development of Christian Doctrine,* was published shortly after his conversion to the Catholic Church. The book served to explain to his many followers the reasons for his change of opinion regarding the Catholic doctrines. He saw in his own experience the experience of the Church as well. As he had grown to clarity of understanding through careful attention to the doctrines of the Church and with the passing of time, so, over time, the Church itself had come to clarify and develop its teachings through careful attention to the word of God and the deposit of faith. As for the individual, he reasoned, so also for the Church: "Time is necessary for the full comprehension and perfection of great ideas."[85]

Drawing on the theological conclusions of Cardinal Newman and citing the more narrowly defined statement of the First Vatican Council,[86] the Fathers of the Second Vatican Council formally introduced the notion of the development of doctrine into the universal magisterium of the Church. "The tradition which comes from the apostles develops in the Church with the help of the Holy Spirit. For there is a growth in the understanding of the realities and the words which have been handed down" (*Dei Verbum*, 8). The Council Fathers cite a variety of ways by which this growth takes place: through contemplation and study of the Scriptures and the deposit of faith on the part of all the faithful of the Church, through a deep and intimate understanding of spiritual experience, and through the preaching and instruction of the bishops who have received the charism of truth through episcopal consecration. Finally, the Council Fathers note that this development takes place over time, for, "as the centuries succeed one another, the Church constantly moves forward toward the fullness of divine truth until the words of God reach their complete fulfillment in her."

The Church in every age, confronting new possibilities and asking new questions, continues to develop a fuller and deeper understanding of the truths of revelation. From the beginning, this was the clear belief of the Johannine commu-

nity, whose Gospel, with reference to the Holy Spirit, quoted
Jesus as saying, "When he comes, being the Spirit of truth,
he will guide you in all truth" (John 16:13). Versed in the
revelation of Jesus and the teaching of his disciples, all the
members of the Church would be led interiorly by the Holy
Spirit to apply the Gospel message to new situations. The
Holy Spirit, the Paraclete sent from the Father, would continue to speak what he hears and announce the things to
come (John 16:13). In times of trial and persecution, the
same Spirit would teach them all that should be said (Lk
12:12; Matt 10:20; Mk 13:11). In the process they would
grow in their understanding of the good news, not a dead
letter but a living witness to the truth revealed in God's only
son. Like Jewish scribes pondering the Torah, searching the
bases for legal judgments, and expanding thereby the significance of the Scriptures, adding precedent to precedent in a
growing awareness of God's revealed will, the followers of
Christ would develop through time an expanded awareness
of the height and breadth and depth of divine revelation.[87]
Not everything would be clear from the beginning. It takes
time for the full understanding of great ideas.

Very early the community of Matthew's Gospel was forced
to confront this reality. The members of this community saw
themselves as the vanguard and embodiment of the reign of
God. They were a community of saints commissioned by the
Lord to make disciples of all nations. Like the tiny mus-
tard seed planted in the ground or the small portion of yeast
that leavens the entire loaf of bread, the reign of God would
spread out from their community to encompass the entire
world. In the beginning, they were a community of Jewish
converts. Following the example of Peter, however, to whom
had been given the keys of the Kingdom of Heaven and

the power to admit new members to the Church, they had opened their doors to an ever increasing number of gentiles (Matt 16:18–20). As the membership of their Church rapidly expanded, they discovered many converts who were not fully committed to living the Christian life. Some defected, while others reverted to their earlier ways of living, despite the fact that they continued to call themselves followers of Christ. Nearly the entire thirteenth chapter of the Gospel is comprised of seven parables about the reign of God, three of them dealing with the eventual separation of those who do not truly belong to God's kingdom. The chapter concludes with Jesus asking his disciples whether they understood the parables he had presented. When they responded that they did, he replied, "Every scribe who is learned in the reign of God is like the head of a household who can bring from his storeroom both the old and the new" (Matt 13:52).

The closing line of the parable instructs the members of the community to expand their awareness of the reign of God. Like something new being fetched from the storeroom, a new teaching about the reign of God was being presented. Did they have the insight to recognize it and the faith to accept it? Did they understand this new teaching? Until the parousia, until the Lord returns at the end of time, the Church must make room for sinners as well as saints, for gentiles and Jews, for slaves and freemen, for the rich and the poor, for women and men, for people of every nation, race, background, and condition under heaven. It's the Church as James Joyce described it: "Here comes everybody." At first, Jesus had instructed his disciples to avoid the gentiles and "go instead after the lost sheep of the house of Israel" (Matt 10:6). Now the Holy Spirit was instructing them to make disciples of all nations, even as Jesus had commanded them at the Ascension (Matt 28:19). The scribe learned in the reign of God had brought forth something new from the storehouse of Scripture and from the deposit of faith.

Jesus' dictum regarding the scribe, however, is not limited to expanding the notion of Church within the reign of God. It applies to all the doctrines of the Church. If the good news is to be vital, dynamic, and relevant in every age, then it must be applied anew in every generation and inculturated in every society. The good news will always be new as well as old. Confronting new situations, there will always be something new to be said, some new application to be made. The scribe inspired by the Spirit of God and searching carefully the pages of Scripture will discern and bring forth what is new whenever it is needed. Matthew 13:52 stands side by side with John 14:26 in expressing the same fundamental truth, that "the Paraclete, the Holy Spirit whom the Father will send in my name, will instruct you in everything and remind you of all that I told you." Our theology is dependent on remembering the faith passed down through the centuries, but it is equally dependent on applying that faith to new circumstances and new situations. Whether it results from the action of a scribe searching the pages of Scripture or of the Paraclete instructing the minds and hearts of the faithful through the preaching of Church leaders, the doctrine of the Church will continue to develop in fidelity to the past and responsiveness to the future. It simply takes time for the full understanding of great ideas.

This truth was not lost on the Fathers of the Church. From the very beginning there was some recognition of doctrinal development, even if the notion itself was not yet clearly developed. Early patristic writers like St. Irenaeus, Tertullian,

Origen, St. Gregory of Nazianzus and St. Basil acknowledged that the truth of Scripture and the implications of doctrine often become more fully explicated with the passing of time. To illustrate this they often resorted to organic images, like the growth of a plant from a seedling or of an adult from an infant. St. Vincent of Lerins well exemplifies this point when he distinguishes between progress and change in the comprehension of doctrine. "What is meant by progress," he writes, "is that something is brought to an advancement from within itself, whereas change denotes a transformation from one thing into another." The doctrine does not change, but with the progress of time and thought its meaning becomes more fully understood. "The progress of religion is like the growth of bodies, which, in the course of years, evolve and develop but still remain what they were."[88] He continues with a second analogy: "Our forefathers sowed the seeds of faith in this field which is the Church." As there is no discrepancy between the seed that is sown and the grain that is harvested, there is also no discrepancy between the "seeds of instruction" and the "fruit of dogma." "Although in the course of time," he concludes, "something evolved from those first seeds and has now expanded under careful cultivation, nothing of the characteristics of the seeds is changed." The essential content of doctrine remains the same.

As noted in the last chapter, St. Vincent of Lerins taught that, as the Church continues to expound upon the doctrines that have been passed down from the apostles by way of public Tradition, those doctrines which formerly are believed with obscurity of understanding later become more clearly understood. "May posterity," he prays, looking to the future, "rejoice in understanding what in times past was venerated without understanding."[89] Origen likewise noted that the apostles, in preaching the faith of Christ, treated with utmost clarity those matters which they believed to be of absolute necessity for all believers, but they left their assertions to be investigated further by those who would receive from the Holy Spirit the gifts of language, wisdom, and knowledge needed for the full elucidation of their teaching.[90]

Perhaps none of the Fathers so clearly states the patristic doctrine of development as does St. Gregory of Nazianzus when he attests that God, in making known the truth, respects our human inability to grasp the fullness of revelation all at once and, therefore, reveals the truth only by degrees. The Old Testament, for example, proclaimed the Father, and the New Testament revealed the Son, but the full divinity of the Holy Spirit became known only over the course of time.

> Our Savior hid some things from his disciples which they could not understand at the time, although they were filled with many more teachings. He foretold that all things would be taught us by the Holy Spirit when he came to dwell among us. Of these things was the very divinity of the Holy Spirit himself. This would be made clear later on, when such knowledge would be seasonable and capable of being accepted, when it would no longer be received with incredulity because of its marvelous character.[91]

Newman also used the principle of organic growth to explain the development of certain Catholic doctrines which seemed only germinally evident in the apostolic period, but which came to full flower at a later time in the Church. Among the numerous illustrations which he cites in the *Essay* are the canon of Scripture, the doctrine of original sin, the consubstantiality of Jesus with the Father, infant baptism, papal supremacy, sacramental grace, purgatory, merit, the veneration of saints, and devotion to Mary. Newman might also have noted the Trinity, as St. Gregory of Nazianzus indicated above, since the doctrine of the Trinity could not be definitively taught until the divinity of the Holy Spirit and the Spirit's consubstantiality with the Father and the Son were clearly defined.

Newman constructed seven pragmatic tests to distinguish legitimate developments from theological distortions:

- consistency with the original teaching: it avoids distorting the meaning of the doctrine it is intended to develop

- coherence with the principles of faith: it does not contradict the basic tenets of Christian belief

- compatibility with other doctrines: like one piece in a larger puzzle, it easily fits in with other doctrines of the Church

- early anticipation of later teaching: traces of this doctrine can be found in the apostolic period

- logical and sequential development: the pattern of development becomes apparent over time

- continued inclusion and preservation of earlier teaching: the earlier teaching is clearly evident in the later doctrine

- meaningful duration over time: the doctrine has had a continuous and dynamic significance for living the Christian life

Above all, Newman considered consistency, antiquity, and coherent development to be the indicators of truth. "The point to be ascertained," he wrote, "is the unity and identity of the idea with itself through all stages of its development from first to last, and these are seven tokens that it may rightly be accounted one and the same all along."[92]

Throughout the *Essay,* Newman cast his definition of doctrinal development in terms of the growth of ideas and the passage of time.

> The view on which it is written has at all times, perhaps, been implicitly adopted by theologians,... that, from the nature of the human mind, time is necessary for the full comprehension and perfection of great ideas; and that the highest and most wonderful truths, though communicated to the world once for all by inspired teachers, could not be comprehended all at once by the recipients, but, as being received and transmitted by minds not inspired and through media which were human, have required only the longer time and deeper thought for their full elucidation. This may be called the *Theory of Development of Doctrine.*[93]

Many theologians today would find Newman's notional/organic understanding of development too narrow and restrictive. His definition implies, if not a propositional approach to revelation, at least the conviction that all doctrine was implicitly contained in the deposit of faith communicated to the apostolic Church and intuitively grasped by the entire Church from the beginning. The apostles, like Jesus himself, are presented as the inspired teachers who received and communicated to the Church the highest truths of divine revelation at once and in their entirety. As such, the deposit of faith has been complete since the beginning, comprehended by the apostles but only obscurely understood by their disciples. Whether one accepts Newman's particular approach to doctrinal development, or one of several other possible approaches offered by various theologians, the truth of his initial insight remains unchallenged: it takes time for the full understanding of great ideas.[94]

Related Doctrines

The notion of development has significance for every major doctrine of Christianity, specifically for those only obscurely and implicitly understood in the apostolic period. For example, it took the Church over four centuries, until the Council of Chalcedon in 451 C.E., to finally clarify the identity of Jesus as a single divine person possessing two distinct natures, hypostatically united yet unconfused, unchangeable, undivided, and inseparable, consubstantial in divinity with the Father and consubstantial in humanity with us. It was not until 381 C.E., at the First Council of Constantinople, that the divinity of the Holy Spirit was defined and the full doctrine of the Holy Spirit received authoritative universal acceptance. Only then could the doctrine of the Trinity be definitely asserted, yet the Trinity is the principal and foundational doctrine of Christianity. Were the Trinity not true doctrine, Jesus would not be divine and we would not be saved. The notion of development, however, has particular impact on certain other doctrines of the Church, namely, sacred Tradition, the role of the faithful in the determination of authentic teaching, the magisterium of bishops, and the infallibility of the Church.

Tradition and Traditions

Before the Gospels were committed to writing or St. Paul had drafted a single letter to the churches he founded, the message of Jesus and the kerygma about him had been preached for several decades and handed on from one community to another by word of mouth. At the same time, prayers, hymns, and concise statements of faith were proclaimed aloud and committed to memory. In subsequent years, the faith that was first communicated orally became the standard for determining the validity of written texts. St. Paul warned the faithful at Galatia to reject any new teaching that did not correspond to the Gospel which they had first received through his preaching (Gal 1:8–9). Through the centuries written commentaries on the word of Scripture, particularly the writings of the Church Fathers, together with the lived experience of faith became standards by which theological opinions often were declared valid or heretical.

Synods and councils of bishops frequently met to hammer out creeds and rules of faith and to sit in judgment on suspect teaching. Liturgy captured the faith of the people and "the norm of praying became the norm of believing." When disputes arose over the interpretation of Scripture, determinations were made by looking back to see what the Church had believed and taught in centuries past. When new situations required fresh solutions and new philosophies forced reformulations of belief, there was assurance in discovering continuity and coherence with earlier expressions of faith. That which the whole Church had always believed became the standard of truth.[95]

As the centuries followed one after another, customs, theological opinions, popular beliefs, and forms of devotion came and went, but what clearly emerged was a consistent standard of belief and a consistent understanding of the faith. Through all these many traditions — prayers, creeds, rites, schools of thought, formulas of faith, written commentaries, oral preaching, codes of law — the foundations of faith emerged as a strong and identifiable Tradition, with a capital "T." Not every custom and expression of faith became a tradition, and not every tradition endured the passage of time, but together with Sacred Scripture, sacred Tradition became identified by the Church as the supreme rule of faith (*Dei Verbum,* 21).

The Second Vatican Council noted the essential connection and dialogue that exists between Scripture and Tradition. Both of them are expressions of the word of God and together form a single deposit of faith. Sacred Scripture is the word of God consigned to writing under the inspiration of the Holy Spirit, and sacred Tradition is the word of God lived out in every generation of the Church under the inspiration of that same divine Spirit. "Consequently, it is not from Sacred Scripture alone that the Church draws her certainty about everything which has been revealed. Both sacred tradition and Sacred Scripture are to be accepted and venerated with the same sense of devotion and reverence" (*Dei Verbum,* 9).

Our understanding of the faith today, like our interpretation of the Scriptures, is essentially linked with the understanding of faith passed down to us through the centuries by the Church. We may not phrase our formulas of belief in exactly the same way that earlier Christians formulated theirs, but unless the content of belief is the same, we have no assurance of living in the same faith which the disciples of Jesus first communicated to their disciples. At the same time, unless our interpretation of Scripture is consistent with the rule of faith lived out in the Church over the centuries, we cannot be assured of believing as the first Christians believed. Both Scripture and Tradition are essential to authentic Christianity, and each must remain in dialogue with the other.

Neither Scripture nor Tradition alone provides a sufficient basis for the sure apprehension of revelation. Without the lived expression of faith which Tradition provides, Scripture becomes a dead letter, a source for researching the past, but hardly the living word of God that nourishes a living faith. Without the oversight of Scripture, Christianity would loose its footing in the apostolic Church and, wandering off in search of new spiritual experience, abandon the continuity of faith which Tradition provides. Without Tradition, Scripture becomes subject to whimsical interpretation. Without Scripture, Tradition is left rudderless, bereft of the most basic formulation of faith connecting the Church of today with the apostolic age of the past. At the same time, Christianity is a dynamic faith. Living within Tradition is not reducible to replicating the past. Faith that is alive cannot avoid involvement in the present. Confronting the new challenges which each age and culture presents, a living faith propels Tradition itself toward greater clarity and connectedness with all the dimensions of a person's life. Aspects of Tradition that were less significant and only implicitly understood in the past may come to greater clarity and more explicit expression at a later period, as faith seeks to meet the needs and challenges of a different age. This was the insight of Cardinal Newman, who recognized that Tradition itself, like individual doctrines, will continue to develop over time as it engages the forces of history.[96] It takes time for the full understanding of great ideas.

Sensus Fidelium

In his short essay *On Consulting the Faithful in Matters of Doctrine* (short by comparison with his *Essay on the Development of Christian Doctrine*), Cardinal Newman makes an interesting comment with reference to the Church of the fourth century:

> It is not a little remarkable, that, though, historically speaking, the fourth century is the age of doctors, illustrated, as it was, by the saints Athanasius, Hilary, the two Gregories, Basil, Chrysostom, Ambrose, Jerome, and Augustine,... nevertheless in that very day the divine tradition committed to the infallible Church was proclaimed and maintained far more by the faithful than by the Episcopate.[97]

His reference, of course, is to the great Christological heresy of Arianism, which, in its various forms, dominated the attention of the Church for some sixty years. Many bishops, monks, and theologians of the time were infected with this heresy and through their teaching led many of the faithful to accept it — but by no means the majority. In the end, Arianism was defeated, not by strong, unified teaching on the part of the bishops, but by the staunch fidelity of the members of the Church. Overwhelmingly, it was the faithful who recognized Arianism for what it was, a denial of the very faith that had been handed down to them from the apostles.

In an attempt to explain how Jesus was both true God and true man, Arius had ended by denying the very divinity of Jesus. At the Council of Nicaea in 325 c.e., the bishops condemned the teachings of Arius, but many in the Church resisted that condemnation. Newman comments further, "The Nicene dogma was maintained during the greater part of the fourth century, not by the unswerving firmness of the Holy See, Councils, or Bishops, but by the *consensus fidelium*,"[98] by which he meant the solidarity of belief demonstrated by all the faithful. Newman is here referring to the unerring ability of the general membership of the Church over the centuries, inspired by the Holy Spirit, to recognize and maintain the truth of faith. It is, as the Second Vatican Council notes, "a supernatural sense of the faith which characterizes the People of God as a whole" (*Lumen Gentium*, 12).

Newman cites this *consensus* or *sensus fidelium* as expressing an essential role for all the faithful of the Church in the determination of authentic teaching. It is not a matter of requiring a vote or taking a poll of the membership before defining Church teaching. The body of the faithful is far more extensive than the membership of any one time. Rather, it is a matter of examining the whole history of the Church to determine what the faithful of every place and time have believed. Despite the fact that doctrines develop over time, the essential core of belief is there from the beginning, although perhaps only implicitly or obscurely understood. Newman states the point effectively in *An Essay on the Development of Christian Doctrine*. Were St. Athanasius or St. Ambrose to return to life today, he argues, despite the fact that many doctrines have developed over the centuries and some doctrines understood only implicitly in their day have since been objectively defined, they would nonetheless be as comfortable and at home in the Catholic Church

of today as they were in the Church of their own time.[99]
This is due to the fact that, sharing in the *sensus fidelium*,
they would recognize the consistency of teaching despite the
development of doctrine.

The *sensus fidelium* was not a new doctrine when Newman argued for its significance in the process of defining
Church teaching. The Council of Trent had already referred
to the "universal understanding of the Church" when it defined the real presence of Christ in the Eucharist.[100] Among
the Fathers of the Church, St. Augustine had spoken of the
importance of that understanding of faith which was held
by all the members of the Church, "from the bishops down
to the last member of the laity."[101] The very term *sensus
fidelium* had been defined in this sense and used over the
centuries by theologians like Albert the Great, Thomas Aquinas, Robert Bellarmine, and Francisco Suarez. The sense of
the faithful is essential to the legitimate development of doctrine. The Church cannot define what the people of God do
not believe. The Holy Spirit, who dwells in the Church and
leads it to the fullness of truth, would not permit it to happen. Often, however, as frequently the history of the Church
has shown to be true, the full understanding of the faithful
and clarity of doctrine unfold slowly. It often takes time for
the full development of great ideas.

Magisterium of the Bishops

The term "magisterium" refers to teaching authority in the
Christian faith. To whom does one listen to understand with
certainty the word of God, to interpret correctly the message of Scripture, and to apply consistently the principles
and dictates of the Christian faith in the individual circum-

stances of life? Obviously, neither Scripture nor the teaching of the apostolic Church provides us with prepared answers for all the issues that we face in the world of today. What did Scripture or the Fathers of the Church say about nuclear war, cryogenics, in vitro fertilization, international finance, the rights of the poor, the social equality of women, immigration, or a host of other twentieth-century issues? At the same time, the principles of Christian living are clearly evident through the doctrines and practices of the Church contained in Scripture and lived out in the faith of Christians down through the centuries. Normally, it should not be all that difficult to apply these principles to contemporary issues; but when those issues become complex and controversial, who, exactly, can speak to us with certainty and with authority? Where is the reliable teacher to be found?

Since the sixteenth century, Protestantism has held to the principle of private judgment and to the role of the individual conscience enlightened by God. Each person of faith, turning to the Scriptures as the source of divine instruction, is expected to find the authority within himself or herself to decide the right course of action whenever new issues arise. Since the beginning of the Christian faith, the Church that early became known as "Catholic"[102] identified the voice of authority with the bishops — with each bishop in his own diocese, with groups of bishops gathered in synod over the churches of an identified region, and with all the bishops gathered in council for the Church universal. Thus, the term "magisterium" became identified with the teaching authority of the bishops who exercise leadership within the Church, interpret the Scriptures for the entire faith community, and apply the principles of Christianity to new issues as they arise.

Catholicism has always been identified with rendering assent and respect to the pronouncements of the local bishop within his own diocese and to the entire company or college of bishops whenever they speak to the whole Church in the ordinary exercise of their authority and leadership over the community. In more serious matters, their authority may rightly demand more than reverence and assent; it may require obedience and submission of faith, as when a doctrine is infallibly defined or taught. Thus, the term "magisterium" has come to be identified both with the collegium of bishops and with the exercise of episcopal authority over doctrine and the practices of faith. As the Second Vatican Council clearly taught, "The order of bishops is the successor to the college of the apostles in teaching authority and pastoral rule" (*Lumen Gentium,* 22). Thus, Catholics are required to render to each pronouncement of their bishops the obedience and respect appropriate to the degree of magisterial authority which the pronouncement has invoked. Even in specific situations where personal dissent may be considered permissible, the norm of due reverence and respect remains in force, guiding the manner and degree of such dissent.

Not only has doctrine continued to develop over the centuries, but the principles of Christian practice have also developed as new issues and circumstances have required new applications of the Christian message and new solutions. In all these areas, the magisterium of the bishops has provided the standard of authority and clarified the rule of faith. Realizing that it takes time for the full understanding of great ideas, the whole people of God is meant to rely on the magisterium of the bishops for clarity of doctrine and assurance in living the Christian faith.

Infallibility of the Church

To speak of infallibility is to speak not of the actions of human beings, but of the action of God. It is God who is infallible, and it is God who chooses to exercise infallibility through the entire community of believers and the leadership of the Church. With great astuteness, Cardinal Newman pointed out that, whereas developments in Christian doctrine are to be expected, such developments cannot be recognized and certified as true unless there exists some authority to whom God has given a guaranteed gift of never erring in the recognition and declaration of truth.[103] This gift is bestowed first of all on the entire people of God who, inspired by the Holy Spirit, cannot err in the recognition of divine truth. The Second Vatican Council expressed this understanding most clearly when it stated, "The body of the faithful as a whole, anointed as they are by the Holy One, cannot err in matters of belief. Thanks to a supernatural sense of the faith which characterizes the People as a whole, it manifests this unerring quality when, 'from the bishops down to the last member of the laity,' it shows universal agreement in matters of faith and morals" (*Lumen Gentium,* 12).

Secondly, this gift of infallibility is bestowed on the entire college of bishops who, inspired by the Holy Spirit, cannot err in the teaching of divine truth when, in union with the bishop of Rome, the bishops collectively intend to teach infallibly. The Second Vatican Council spoke to this point when it stated,

> Although the individual bishops do not enjoy the prerogative of infallibility, they can nevertheless proclaim Christ's doctrine infallibly. This is so, even when they are dispersed around the world, provided that while

maintaining the bond of unity among themselves and with Peter's successor, and while teaching authentically on a matter of faith or morals, they concur in a single viewpoint as the one which must be held conclusively. (*Lumen Gentium,* 25)

This becomes even more apparent when the pope and bishops gathered in an ecumenical council declare a doctrine of the Church to be infallibly defined. Finally, the bishop of Rome, in his capacity as supreme shepherd of the universal Church and speaking as head of the entire college of bishops, exercises the gift of infallibility for the entire Church when he declares a doctrine of faith or morals to be infallibly defined. In such a case, as the Council Fathers clearly taught, "the Roman Pontiff is not pronouncing judgment as a private person. Rather, as the supreme teacher of the universal Church, as one in whom the charism of the infallibility of the Church herself is individually present, he is expounding or defending a doctrine of Catholic faith" (*Lumen Gentium,* 25). In every case, the exercise of infallibility does not add new revelation to the body of beliefs expounded by the Church. The whole people of God does not admit "that there could be any new public revelation pertaining to the divine deposit of faith" (*Lumen Gentium,* 25). Rather, linked with the notion of doctrinal development, the gift of infallibility guarantees that true doctrine will always be recognized universally throughout the Church and authoritatively declared without error. Doctrines, like great ideas, necessarily develop over time. Only the Holy Spirit, the infallible custodian of truth, can guarantee that the doctrines of Christ are infallibly developed, received, and taught within the community of the Church.

Implications for an Applied Theology

The teachings of Christ and the doctrines of the Church continue to develop over time as human language evolves, human thought expands, and human experience unfolds. The encounter of Christian doctrine with new philosophies, new cultures, and new languages has always forced the Church to look again at its teaching and find new and more effective ways of expressing the faith in a different context. As the scribe learned in the reign of God and as the custodian of the deposit of faith, the Church must continually bring forth, from the storeroom of revelation, interpretations both old and new. At times there is resistance even to that change which is necessary for the preservation of truth. At the same time, change which is not guided by the Holy Spirit may very well corrupt the truth of revelation. Both immutable resistance and heedless change divide the people of God and do irreparable harm to the body of Christ. To recognize that great ideas require time for their full development is to recognize the validity of change that is appropriate and guided. Cardinal Newman spoke to this point when he wrote,

> Whatever be the risk of corruption from intercourse with the world around, such a risk must be encountered if a great idea is duly to be understood, and much more if it is to be fully exhibited. . . . Old principles reappear under new forms. [The great idea] changes with them in order to remain the same. In a higher world it is otherwise, but here below to live is to change, and to be perfect is to have changed often.[104]

How we approach change in the development of doctrine has serious implications for the formulation of Church teaching, the rejection of Integralism, and the work of theology.

Dogmatic Formulas

Language changes over time as words change their meanings. We need only consult any dictionary of the English language to note the frequency with which words are defined with an archaic meaning as well as a contemporary one. Language is used to define doctrine. If we are not careful to note the changes in linguistic meaning, we may distort or even alter the doctrinal definitions of the Church and end up believing that our own understanding is the correct one. In fact, it may not be. One frequently noted example of this is the way in which the theological terms "person" and "nature" have differed between their use in patristic theology and the way they are understood today. Careful to distinguish "personality" from "personhood," we still tend to think of the human person in psychological rather than philosophical terms. Moreover, we think of "person" as an individual's dynamic center of human activity. By contrast, we view "nature" as the rather passive essence or constitutive quality of something or of someone. We speak of the nature of democracy, the nature of a particular breed of dog, human nature in general, or of our own particular nature, as in the expression, "It's my nature to act this way."

In the patristic period, when the great Councils of Nicaea, Constantinople, and Chalcedon defined the "two natures" in Christ and the "three persons" in the Trinity, the two terms were used in exactly the opposite way from the way they are used today. At that time "nature" designated the dynamic center of activity, while "person" defined the individuation of the essence or constitutive quality which several like beings held in common. The change in terminology, of course, has enormous impact on our understanding of the one person of Jesus Christ, a divine person not a human one, who exists in two natures, human and divine. It also impacts our understanding of the three Persons of the Trinity. The correct understanding of doctrine requires a careful analysis of the original language used and an awareness of the intent of the original formulators of the definition. Simply to quote the doctrinal formula of a past pope or council of the Church is no guarantee that what was defined then will be correctly understood today.

This problem is compounded when we translate our teaching from one language into another. Culture determines the meaning of words. The same word used by people of two different cultures may have significantly different connotations. At times there may not be an equivalent word in another language, making the translation that much more difficult. The churches of the East and West have long experienced this problem with the term "substance" as it is used in both Christology and the theology of the Trinity. The Greek term was *ousia,* which Latin theologians translated as *substantia* and English translates as "substance." In order to express the equality and likeness of the three Persons of the Trinity to each other, the Greek-speaking Eastern Fathers spoke of *homoousias* and the Latin-speaking Western Fathers spoke of *consubstantia.* In English we have translated both words as "consubstantial." However, the Eastern Fathers saw the *ousia* of God as belonging to the Father and as shared in by the Son and the Holy Spirit. They are separately consubstantial with the Father. In the West, *substantia* was understood as belonging to all three Persons, almost as if it was an entity unto itself which all three shared equally. This, in turn, led to the never resolved debate of the Eastern and Western churches: does the Holy Spirit proceed from the Father *through* the Son, as Orthodoxy claims, or from the Father *and* the Son, as Catholicism has defined? It may seem like only a problem of terminology, but, in part because of this issue, the Orthodox and Catholic churches have remained separated for nearly a thousand years.

Philosophical language likewise presents a difficulty for the average member of the Church who has not been educated in the principles, theories, and terminology of the several philosophical systems in which doctrine has been defined and explained over the centuries. The term "substance," for example, which has enormous importance for understanding the Eucharistic doctrine as defined by the Council of Trent, offers a real challenge to contemporary believers who interpret the word almost exclusively in terms of physical materiality. The most frequent usage of the term associates substance with the physical properties of matter. As the Church has discovered from long experience, unless the formulas of faith are expressed in the language and philosophy that the people of each time and culture implicitly understand, these people may be baptized, but they will not be truly catechized.

It is never sufficient to simply pass on the doctrinal formulas of the past. The correct understanding of doctrine often requires that new formulas be developed, faithful to the meaning of the past but not frozen by the language of the past. When members of the faithful argue over the question of fidelity to the Church, to the Tradition, or to the magisterium, when they cite the doctrinal formulas of popes and councils, when they resurrect the *anathemas* of the past in language that may carry very different connotations from today, before they turn their backs on one another and walk away, before they destroy the unity and charity of the Church, it is most important that they recognize the limitations of language and seek common ground through theological research. It takes time for the full understanding of great ideas. Time also requires the faithful reformulation of past statements of faith.

Integralism

Pope John Paul II has warned against what is termed the "heresy of Integralism." Integralism first developed in France in the late nineteenth century as an organized movement to protect against the possibility of doctrinal deviations in Catholic teaching. Theologians, biblical scholars, and even bishops whose pronouncements were considered dangerous to the faith often found themselves discredited and denounced. In turn, Pope Benedict XV, in his first encyclical letter, denounced the practices of the Integralists.[105] Thereafter, the organized form of Integralism died out, but its tendencies continually reappear in movements that seek to discourage theological inquiry and to suppress ideas judged contrary to Tradition.

Integralism presents itself as the defender of orthodoxy, but instead masks a contempt for truth by slavishly restating the formulas of faith without distinction, nuance, or insight. In a letter to Cardinal Joseph Ratzinger that appeared in *L'Osservatore Romano* in 1988, Pope John Paul described Integralism as a theological position or tendency that "stops at the past itself without taking into account the correct aspiration towards the future." Such an approach "sees correctness only in what is ancient, considering it synonymous with Tradition."[106] The words of the pope echo those of Cardinal Newman more than a century earlier, "One cause of corruption in religion is the refusal to follow the course of doctrine as it moves on, and an obstinacy in the notions of the past."[107]

St. Augustine opposed an early form of Integralism as it appeared in his day. He wrote that he was often grieved and dismayed that the weak in faith were so greatly disturbed by the obstinate aggressiveness and unfounded warnings of certain members of the community. These members, he said, stirred up controversial questions and accepted nothing as correct except that which conformed to their own customary beliefs and practices. Often these were practices not prescribed by the authority of Scripture nor by the Tradition of the universal Church and were not essential for the amending of one's life.[108] Those of every age who recognize the work of the Holy Spirit in the unfolding of Tradition will not cling obstinately to notions of the past. Rather, they will look for signs of continuity between the implicit beliefs of the apostolic age and the developed doctrines of the later Church.

Theology

Three periods of considerable theological growth in the development of doctrine can be readily identified. The first was the patristic period, when the revelation of Christianity found new expression through the encounter with Hellenistic philosophy. The Apologists and the Fathers of the Church sought to work out the philosophical implications of the

Christian message and to refute intellectual attacks against the faith. In the wedding of philosophy and theology that took place in the writings of St. Augustine, the Church produced a theological approach that endured for more than eight hundred years. In the second great period, the scholastic writers of the twelfth and thirteenth centuries produced a systematic theology based on newly acquired philosophical understandings. The aim of their theology was to integrate all the data of revelation into a single system capable of responding to every inquiry and challenge that philosophical criticism could produce. The Thomistic-Aristotelian synthesis that resulted provided a bulwark for Church doctrine in the face of the challenges raised by the sixteenth-century Reformation theologians. It was a system of theology that dominated the Church for four centuries. The third period of growth began in the middle of the last century and continues today. It is a period of examining once again the sources and data of revelation in the light of advanced sciences and technologies and responding to the inquiries raised by new philosophical approaches and cultural encounters. Perhaps there has never been a period of such rapid expansion of knowledge as we are experiencing in the world in which we presently live. The end result for theology is yet to be seen.

Theology is not catechesis. Its purpose is not simply to impart doctrine and form faithful members of the Church. Theology does more than clarify the faith and make it understandable. The work of theology is to expand the circle of truth while holding firmly to the center, to stretch the envelope of faith by making new inquiries and asking new questions, to discover the unforeseen implications that arise whenever new philosophical schools of thought challenge established doctrines and beliefs. Theology looks for connections between revelation, on the one hand, and science, philosophy, and the arts, on the other. Theology also looks for connections between the various doctrines that arise from revelation and that exist between the teaching and the practice of the faith.

While there is only one faith, there are many possible theologies. Within the limits defined by doctrine, there is sufficient room for the diversity of theological opinion that allows doctrine itself to develop. The Church has always honored a variety of theological schools, methodologies, and systems, subjecting each one to the same test of Scripture and Tradition. Each theology is valid to the degree that it preserves the data of revelation and integrates that data into a single, comprehensive system. Only those who have the courage to ask questions and the persistence to pursue them are ready and competent to do the work of theology. This is always a dangerous task. It involves uncovering the face of God. Mistakes can be made. False teachings can arise. Faith can be tested. But the truth, faithfully sought after and faithfully adhered to, will set us free (John 8:32). To do the work of theology requires great care, great reverence, and great love. It also requires patience. It takes time for the full understanding of great ideas.

Notes

1. T. S. Eliot, "Little Gidding," part V, from "Four Quartets," in *The Complete Poems and Plays, 1909–1950* (New York: Harcourt, Brace and World, 1952), 145.

2. In *Catholicism: Christ and the Common Destiny of Man* (1947), Henri de Lubac correctly argues that this notion is the distinguishing doctrine of the Catholic faith, that it is clearly evident in Scripture and in the writings of the Fathers of the Church, and that it permeates a correct understanding of all Church teaching from the earliest days of Christianity. Throughout the text and in the appendices, de Lubac supports his argument by citing numerous extracts from the writings of the Church Fathers. A recent edition of this work is available from Ignatius Press (San Francisco, 1988).

3. Among the Scripture texts frequently cited is 1 Corinthians 15:21–24. In context, St. Paul is defending faith in the resurrection of believers, citing the fact that with Adam's sin all human beings have become subject to death, but through the redemptive action of Christ all shall be made alive. According to St. Paul, this restoration of life is progressive, beginning with Christ and those who belong to him, but eventually leading to the final destruction of death itself. Alexander of Alexandria, among other Christian Fathers, understood this teaching to have a wider application to the entire doctrine of redemption and the eventual restoration of that unity which was destroyed by the sin of Adam. See *Sermon on the Soul and Body and on the Passion of Christ* 7 (PG 18, 602–3).

4. The Fathers of the Church, in particular the Greek Fathers, preferred the term "divinization" when speaking of our incorporation in Christ. Divinization is more than being made holy. It is more than living the life of grace. Divinization involves the whole life of the Trinity. The Trinity indwells us in that our human nature is transformed by the Spirit, configured to Christ, and united

with the Father. We do not become God or part of God, but we do become more than God-like. According to Theodore of Mopsuestia, "We enter into a share of the divine nature" (*Sixth Liturgical Homily*, quoted in de Lubac, *Catholicism,* 389).

5. Origen, *On Ezekiel* 9, 1 (PG 13, 732).

6. St. Cyril of Alexandria, *On John the Evangelist* 1, 14 (PG 73, 161–64); St. Hilary, *On the Trinity* 2, 25 (PL 10, 67).

7. St. Irenaeus, *Against Heresies* 4, 20, 7 (PG 7, 1037).

8. Two further questions follow closely upon the first two: Is salvation at all possible for the atheist who has rejected not only fellowship in the Church but even belief in God's own Son; and if possible, how is the Church involved in the salvation of those who have consciously rejected the mediation of Christ and of the Church? The question of the salvation of the atheist is being raised increasingly among theologians today and deserves particular attention that cannot be given to it here. See, for example, Karl Rahner, "Atheism and Implicit Christianity," *Theological Investigations* 9, 145–64; "Anonymous and Explicit Faith," *Theological Investigations* 16, 52–59; "The Church and Atheism," *Theological Investigations* 21, 137–50.

9. Belief in the universal salvific will of God raises the thorny question of the fate of those who, through personal sin, reject the grace of Christ. Is it possible that no one is condemned, even those who commit the most heinous offenses and reject all standards of morality? The question of the universal salvific will of God has been explored by such notable theologians as Hans Urs von Balthasar, *Dare We Hope That All Men Be Saved?* (San Francisco: Harper and Row, 1988); Karl Rahner, "Anonymous Christians," *Theological Investigations* 6, 390–98; Karl Barth, *Dogmatics in Outline* (London: SCM Press, 1949), 118–20, 134–36; and Francis A. Sullivan, *Salvation Outside the Church?* (New York: Paulist Press, 1992).

10. In the Fourth Eucharistic Prayer of the Roman Liturgy, the Church addresses the Father in these words, "Remember those who have died in the peace of Christ and all the dead whose faith is known to you alone."

11. The contemporary understanding of the Church as the instrument of universal and integral salvation, coupled with a carefully argued theological explanation for the Church as the

medium of salvific grace operative in the world, is offered by Francis A. Sullivan, *The Church We Believe In* (New York: Paulist Press, 1988).

12. Second Vatican Council, Dogmatic Constitution on the Church (*Lumen Gentium*), 48.

13. Second Vatican Council, Pastoral Constitution on the Church in the Modern World (*Gaudium et Spes*), 45.

14. Second Vatican Council, Decree on the Missionary Activity of the Church (*Ad Gentes*), 1.

15. The Second Vatican Council, in the Constitution on the Sacred Liturgy (*Sacrosanctum Concilium*), in two passages boldly asserts that the grace of salvation continues to be present in the world through the Eucharistic Sacrifice. "For it is through the liturgy, especially the divine Eucharistic Sacrifice, that 'the work of our redemption is exercised' " (article 2). "From the liturgy, therefore, and especially from the Eucharist, as from a fountain, grace is channeled into us; and the sanctification of men in Christ and the glorification of God, to which all other activities of the Church are directed as toward their goal, are most powerfully achieved" (article 10).

16. Second Vatican Council, Decree on Ecumenism (*Unitatis Redintegratio*), 3.

17. The historical development of the Church's understanding of the salvation of non-believers, especially with reference to the maxim, "Outside the Church there is no salvation," is carefully detailed by Francis A. Sullivan in *Salvation Outside the Church?*

18. St. Augustine, *Popular Sermons* 341, 9 (PL 39, 1499–1500).

19. On this point, see St. Justin Martyr, *First Apology for Christians* 46 (PG 6, 397).

20. Origen, *Homily on the Birth of Jesus* 3.5 (PG 12, 841–42).

21. The response of St. Augustine to the adherents of Donatism is illustrative of the importance of the Church for the salvation of the individual. Among their teachings, the Donatists claimed that a bishop who was himself guilty of sin could not absolve from sin, neither through baptizing nor through readmitting those who had been separated from the Church. In response, St. Augustine maintained that it was through the power of the Church itself that the sinner is absolved and restored to the grace of salvation that had

been lost through sin. Moreover, he maintained it is solely because the Church, with an innate holiness derived from its attachment to Christ, continues to be present in the world that the power to restore the sinner to salvation also continues to be present in the world. In short, the grace of salvation is made available to the individual in and through the community of the Church. See *Teaching on Baptism against the Opinions of the Donatists* 3, 18, 23 (PL 43, 150). Although the Church was later to define that the power of absolution properly belongs to the bishop and presbyter by ordination, the force of St. Augustine's argument here supports his belief in salvation within community.

22. Council of Florence, "Decree for the Jacobites" (DS 1351).

23. See Domingo Soto, *De natura et gratia* II, 12 (Paris, 1549), 148–49.

24. See Francisco de Vitoria, *De indis et de iure belli relectiones* (1539), ed. Ernest Nys, trans. John P. Bate (Buffalo, N.Y: W. S. Hein, 1995), 144, 250, 372.

25. "Letter of the Holy Office to the Archbishop of Boston" (August 8, 1949), quoted in *The Christian Faith in the Doctrinal Documents of the Catholic Church,* ed. J. Neuner and J. Dupuis (Glasgow: Collins, 1983), 240–42. Nearly twenty years later, Father Leonard Feeney was readmitted to the Roman Catholic Church and died in union with Rome. Echoing the original significance of the expression, his gravestone is inscribed with the words, *Extra Ecclesiam Nulla Salus,* "Outside the Church, No Salvation."

26. In the nineteenth century, Friedrich Schleiermacher argued that it was on the perennial strength of Jesus' image as the absolute bearer of divine consciousness that he continues in his role as universal savior (*The Christian Faith* [Edinburgh: T. & T. Clark, 1928], n. 100). Until recently, this position had been largely discredited by the reaction of such important figures within Protestant theology as Karl Barth, Emil Brunner, and Wolfhart Pannenberg. However, one result of the conclusions of notable theologians associated with the contemporary Jesus Seminar, in their attempt to identify the historical figure of Jesus liberated from all theological accretion, has also been the depersonalization of the Christ of faith and a return to an abstract construct of salvation. See, for example, Marcus Borg, *Meeting Jesus Again for the First Time: The Histor-*

ical Jesus and the Heart of Contemporary Faith (San Francisco: Harper and Row, 1994).

27. Attributed to St. Basil, *Letters* 189, 7 (PG 32, 693).

28. A very clear exposition of this principle is found in St. Augustine's letter to Bishop Boniface regarding infant baptism. "Infants are presented for the reception of spiritual grace, not so much by those in whose arms they are carried, although they are offered by them if they are good and faithful people, as by the whole company of the saints and believers. We correctly understand that they are presented by all who consent to the presentation, and by whose holy and indivisible charity they are assisted in sharing in the outpouring of the Holy Spirit" (*Letters* 98, 5 [PL 33, 362]).

29. The history of infant baptism in early Christianity is thoroughly researched and explicated by Joachim Jeremias, *Infant Baptism in the First Four Centuries* (London: SCM Press, 1960).

30. According to the Second Vatican Council, *Lumen Gentium*, 11, the source and summit of the whole Christian life is participation in the celebration of the Eucharist. In proposing this theological notion, the Council Fathers did not limit the Eucharist to its reservation or to the reception of Communion, but focused on the celebration of the Mass as the highest expression of liturgy. This is correctly argued by David N. Power, *The Eucharistic Mystery* (New York: Crossroad, 1993).

31. "Liturgical services are not private functions, but are celebrations of the Church, which is the 'sacrament of unity,' namely, a holy people united and organized under their bishops" (*Sacrosanctum Concilium*, 26). "It is to be stressed that whenever rites, according to their specific nature, make provision for communal celebration involving the presence and active participation of the faithful, this way of celebrating them is to be preferred, as far as possible, to a celebration that is individual and quasi-private. This rule applies with special force to the celebration of Mass and the administration of the sacraments, even though every Mass has of itself a public and social nature" (article 27).

32. Second Preface for Lent from the Roman Liturgy.

33. In other writings, St. Paul further develops this notion of supernatural transformation, notably in Romans 8:1–17 and Colossians 3:1–4.

34. St. Athanasius, *The Incarnation of the Word* 3–5 (PG 25,

101–5); St. Gregory of Nyssa, *The Great Catechism* 5 (PG 45, 20–25).

35. St. Clement of Alexandria, *Miscellaneous Notes on Revealed Knowledge* 6, 12 (PG 9, 318); Origen, *First Principles* 3, 6.1 (PG 11, 333).

36. St. Irenaeus, *Against Heresies* 3, 18, 7 (PG 7, 937–38); 4, 38, 4 (PG 7, 1108–9).

37. Karl Rahner, for example, holds that, from the beginning, human beings were not endowed with the supernatural condition but were certainly created for the possibility of communion with God. In fact, he states, the very condition of our humanity requires it. Therefore, he argues, the possibility of receiving the divine self-communication requires that all human beings be gifted by God with the capacity or disposition for receiving the supernatural order which their natural state could not alone sustain. Rahner refers to this preconditioned capacity for receiving the supernatural as the "supernatural existential." See "Concerning the Relationship Between Nature and Grace," *Theological Investigations* 1, 297–317.

38. St. Augustine, *On the Perfection of Human Justice* 2, 1 (PL 44, 293); 9, 20 (PL 44, 501–2). See also *Against Two Letters of the Pelagians, to Boniface* 1, 2, 5 (PL 44, 552); 3, 8, 24 (PL 44, 606–7).

39. Third Preface for Sundays in Ordinary Time from the Roman Liturgy.

40. St. Anselm, *Cur Deus Homo* 1:1 in *Opera Omnia* (Edinburgh: Nelson and Sons, 1946), 2:47–49; St. Thomas Aquinas, *Summa Theologica*, III, q. 1, a. 3; Walter Kasper, *Jesus the Christ* (New York: Paulist Press, 1977), 185–92, 219–25.

41. John Duns Scotus, *Reportata Parisiensia* 1, 41 in *Opera Omnia* (Paris: Vives, 1894) XXII, 479–82; Karl Rahner, *Sacramentum Mundi* (New York: Herder and Herder, 1969), 3:117–18; Hans Urs von Balthasar, *A Theology of History* (New York: Sheed and Ward, 1963), 62–63; Michael Schmaus, *Dogma 1: God and Revelation* (New York: Sheed and Ward, 1968), 47–51. More recently, von Balthasar wrote that whether Christ became human solely for our redemption or whether his predestination was to become incarnate under any conditions cannot finally be settled, since Scripture always views the two aspects together. Christ came both

as Redeemer and as the final Revelation of the Father, predestined from the creation of the world to offer humankind the fullness of all divine goods and not solely to remit the guilt of sin. *Theo-drama* (San Francisco: Ignatius Press, 1992), 3:253–54. Nonetheless, it is clear that von Balthasar continued to lean toward the view of Duns Scotus, which he more openly supported in his earlier work, *A Theology of History.*

42. St. Augustine wrote extensively on the topic of grace, particularly in his disputes with the Pelagians. See, for example, *Proceedings of Pelagius* (PL 44) and *Against Two Pelagian Letters, to Boniface* (PL 44). His theology is further delineated in his commentaries on Scripture, in particular, *Exposition on the Epistle to the Romans* (PL 35), *Exposition on the Epistle to the Galatians* (PL 35), *Expositions on the Psalms* (PL 36 and 37), and his *Sermons on John* (PL 35), as well as in tracts devoted entirely to the issue of grace, *The Grace of Christ and Original Sin* (PL 44), *Nature and Grace* (PL 44), and *Admonition and Grace* (PL 44).

43. St. Athanasius, *The Incarnation of the Word* 54 (PG 25, 191); St. Leo the Great, *Sermons* 25.5 (PL 54, 211).

44. Karl Menninger, *Whatever Became of Sin?* (New York: Hawthorne Books, 1973). Although written from a psychological perspective, this significant work raises important issues for moral theology and for daily Christian living.

45. St. Therese of Lisieux, "Conversation of June 5, 1897," reported in *Her Last Conversations,* trans. John Clarke (Washington, D.C.: ICS Publications, 1977), 57. On October 19, 1997, Pope John Paul II proclaimed St. Therese a "Doctor of the Church." Of the thirty-three saints to be honored with this title, St. Therese is only the third woman, the others being St. Teresa of Avila and St. Catherine of Siena.

46. Garrison Keillor, *Lake Wobegon Days* (New York: Viking Press, 1985).

47. St. Irenaeus, *Against Heresies* 4, 37, 6 (PG 7, 1103).

48. St. Irenaeus, *Against Heresies* 3, 20, 2 (PG 7, 943–44).

49. St. Irenaeus, *Against Heresies* 4, 37, 1 (PG 7, 1099).

50. St. Clement of Alexandria, *Who Is the Rich Man That Is Saved?* 21, 1 (PG 9, 626).

51. St. Augustine, *Various Questions to Simplician* 1, 2, 13 (PL

40, 119); see also *Forgiveness and the Just Punishment of Sin and the Baptism of Infants* 2, 17, 26 (PL 44, 167).

52. St. Augustine, *Various Questions to Simplician* 1, 2, 14 (PL 40, 119).

53. St. Thomas Aquinas, *Summa Theologica* I, q. 84, aa. 6–7.

54. David Tracy, *The Analogical Imagination* (New York: Crossroad, 1987), 405–38.

55. See St. Thomas Aquinas, *Summa Theologica* I, q. 12, a. 12.

56. Second Vatican Council, Dogmatic Constitution on Divine Revelation (*Dei Verbum*), 5.

57. DS 1306, 1307, 1308.

58. DS 1685, 1709.

59. DS 1673, 1676.

60. DS 1678.

61. This is the particular insight of Karl Rahner and the title of his seminal and major work, first published in 1939. The human person is the only created being with absolute transcendence toward God and the only created being which, as spirit incarnate in the world, apprehends intelligible being through the medium of the senses. Because human subjectivity functions within the horizon of being which has God as its ultimate determinant, the human person understands and interprets the world with a pre-apprehension towards God. See *Spirit in the World* (New York: Herder and Herder, 1968).

62. "God's Grandeur," *Poems of Gerard Manley Hopkins*, 3d ed. (New York: Oxford University Press, 1948), 70.

63. See Elizabeth Johnson, "Turn to the Heavens and the Earth: Retrieval of the Cosmos in Theology," *Proceedings of the Catholic Theological Society of America* 51 (1996): 5.

64. St. Thomas Aquinas, *Summa Theologica*, I, q. 47, a. 1.

65. St. Augustine, *Free Choice* I, 14, 30–I, 16, 36 (PL 32, 1237–40); II, 14, 37 (PL 32, 1261).

66. St. Augustine, *Grace and Free Choice* 15, 31 (PL 44, 899–900).

67. St. Thomas Aquinas, *Summa Theologica* III, q. 80, a. 3.

68. Pontifical Biblical Commission, "The Historical Truth of the Gospels" (1964).

69. Origen, *First Principles* 1, Preface, 2 (PG 11, 116).

70. Tertullian, *The Objection against Heretics* 19 (PL 2, 36).

71. St. Irenaeus, *Against Heresies* 4, 33, 8 (PG 7, 1077).

72. St. Augustine, *Against Julian, Defender of the Pelagian Heresy* 2, 10, 33 (PL 44, 696–97); 1, 7, 30 (PL 44, 661–62).

73. St. Vincent of Lerins, *Commonitoria* 28 (PL 50, 676).

74. St. Vincent of Lerins, *Commonitoria* 2 (PL 50, 639).

75. Edgar Hennecke and Wilhelm Schneemelcher, *New Testament Apocrypha* (Philadelphia: Westminster Press, 1963), 1:42–45.

76. The list of texts recorded by St. Athanasius in his "Easter Letter" of 367 C.E. is the earliest exact witness to the present New Testament canon. The Septuagint, which dates in its final form from the first century B.C.E., was accepted early on by the Christian churches as the official Old Testament canon. It was not until April 8, 1545, that the Council of Trent declared the entire canon of Scripture, both Old and New Testaments, to be definitively closed.

77. St. Cyril of Jerusalem, *Catechetical Lectures* 4, 34 (PG 33, 498).

78. Council of Laodicea, canon 59, in J. D. Mansi, *Sacrorum conciliorum nova et amplissima collectio* (Paris: Huberto Welter, 1901), 2:590.

79. St. Augustine, *Against an Adversary of the Law and the Prophets* 1, 20, 39 (PL 42, 626); see also *Christian Instruction* 2, 8, 12 (PL 34, 40).

80. Tertullian, *Against Marcion* 4, 5 (PL 2, 395).

81. St. Epiphanius of Salamis, *Panacea against Eighty Heresies* 61, 6 (PG 41, 1047).

82. Second Vatican Council, Decree on the Ministry and Life of Priests (*Presbyterorum Ordinis*) 5; *Sacrosanctum Concilium*, 10.

83. St. Augustine, *Against Faustus the Manichean* 11, 5 (PL 42, 249).

84. An indispensable resource for understanding the various stages of biblical tradition is the 1964 Instruction of the Pontifical Biblical Commission, "The Historical Truth of the Gospels," available with commentary in Joseph A. Fitzmyer, *A Christological Catechism*, revised and expanded edition (New York: Paulist Press, 1991), 119–64.

85. John Henry Newman, *An Essay on the Development*

of Christian Doctrine (Westminster, Md.: Christian Classics, 1968), 29.

86. First Vatican Council, Dogmatic Constitution on the Catholic Faith, chapter 4 (DS 3020).

87. The role of the Jewish scribe was to interpret the will of God as embodied in the Scriptures and to study and transmit the ongoing interpretations of the law. The process involves Halakah, a legal decision regarding a matter or case for which there is no direct precedent in the Mosaic law. The decision, deduced by analogy, is included as a binding precept in the Mishna, the collection of binding precepts which forms the core of the Talmud. In this way, the deposit of the Mosaic law continues to develop through newly binding interpretations.

88. St. Vincent of Lerins, *Commonitoria* 23 (PL 50, 668).

89. St. Vincent of Lerins, *Commonitoria* 22 (PL 50, 667).

90. Origen, *First Principles* 1, preface, 3 (PG 11, 116).

91. Gregory of Nazianzus, *Fifth Theological Oration* 31, 27 (PG 36, 164).

92. Newman, *An Essay on the Development,* 206.

93. Newman, *An Essay on the Development,* 29–30.

94. Avery Dulles summarizes three basic approaches to doctrinal development which he identifies as "logical," "organic," and "historical situationist." He offers a brief analysis of each approach in *The Resilient Church* (New York: Doubleday, 1977), 45–62.

95. When St. Vincent of Lerins wrote, "In the Catholic Church herself every care must be taken that we may hold fast to that which has been believed everywhere, always and by all," he formulated the threefold test of orthodoxy that became widely accepted in later centuries. See *Commonitoria* 2 (PL 50, 640).

96. In the *Essay,* Newman differentiates between Christianity as a universal religion (Tradition) and the particular religious practices and individual doctrines that pertain to it. Not only do religious practices evolve and doctrines develop, but Christianity itself "cannot but vary in its relations and dealings toward the world around it, that is, it will develop" (58).

97. John Henry Newman, *On Consulting the Faithful in Matters of Doctrine* (1871), ed. John Coulson (London: Collins, 1986), 75.

98. Newman, *On Consulting the Faithful*, 77.

99. Newman, *An Essay on the Development*, 97–98.

100. The Council of Trent cited the *universus ecclesiae sensus* (universal sense of the Church) in its first chapter of the Decree on the Most Holy Eucharist (DS 1637).

101. St. Augustine, *The Predestination of the Saints* 14, 27 (PL 44, 980).

102. St. Ignatius of Antioch, who asserted the authority of bishops in a series of letters written at the end of the first century and the beginning of the second, is considered to be the first of the Fathers to apply the adjective "Catholic" to the Church found in the apostolic period (*Epistle to the Smyrnians* 8 [PG 5, 714]).

103. Newman, *An Essay on the Development*, 75–92.

104. Newman, *An Essay on the Development*, 39–40.

105. Benedict XV, *Ad Beatissimi Apostolorum* (1914), 21–23.

106. *L'Osservatore Romano,* English ed., 16 (1035) April 18, 1988, 2. In the same letter, the Holy Father offered a warning against the equally destructive "error of Progressivism," which he described as "an aspiration toward the future which breaks with the past, without taking into account the function of Tradition."

107. Newman, *An Essay on the Development*, 177.

108. St. Augustine, "Letter to Januarius," *Letters* 54, 2, 3 (PL 33, 201).

Bibliography

Brennan, John P. *Christ, the One Sent.* Collegeville, Minn.: Liturgical Press, 1997.

Brown, Raymond E. *An Introduction to the New Testament.* New York: Doubleday, 1997.

Chauvet, Louis Marie. *Symbol and Sacrament: A Sacramental Reinterpretation of Christian Existence.* Trans. Patrick Madigan and Madeleine Beaumont. Collegeville, Minn.: Liturgical Press, 1995.

Congar, Yves M.-J. *Tradition and Traditions: An Historical and Theological Essay.* Trans. Michael Naseby and Thomas Rainborough. New York: Macmillan and Company, 1966.

Cooke, Bernard J. *Sacraments and Sacramentality.* 2d ed., rev. Mystic, Conn.: Twenty-Third Publications, 1994.

de Lubac, Henri. *Catholicism: Christ and the Common Destiny of Man.* San Francisco: Ignatius Press, 1988.

Duffy, Stephen J. *The Dynamics of Grace.* Collegeville, Minn.: Liturgical Press, 1993.

Dulles, Avery. *The Catholicity of the Church.* Oxford: Clarendon Press, 1985.

————. *The Craft of Theology.* New York: Crossroad, 1992.

Farmer, William R., and Denis M. Farkasfalvy. *The Formation of the New Testament Canon.* New York: Paulist Press, 1983.

Fischer, Kathleen R., and Thomas N. Hart. *Christian Foundations: An Introduction to Faith in Our Time.* Rev. ed. New York: Paulist Press, 1995.

Flannery, Austin, general editor. *Vatican Council II: The Conciliar and Post Conciliar Documents.* Collegeville, Minn.: Liturgical Press, 1975.

Goizueta, Roberto S. *Caminemos con Jesús: Toward a Hispanic/Latino Theology of Accompaniment.* Maryknoll, N.Y.: Orbis Books, 1995.

Haight, Roger. *The Experience and Language of Grace.* New York: Paulist Press, 1979.

Hellwig, Monika K. *Understanding Catholicism.* New York: Paulist Press, 1981.

Johnson, Elizabeth A. *Consider Jesus: Waves of Renewal in Christology.* New York: Crossroad, 1992.

LaCugna, Catherine Mowry, ed. *Freeing Theology: The Essentials of Theology in Feminist Perspective.* San Francisco: HarperCollins, 1993.

LaCugna, Catherine Mowry. *God for Us: The Trinity and Christian Life.* San Francisco: Harper Collins, 1991.

Newman, John Henry. *An Essay on the Development of Christian Doctrine.* Westminster, Md.: Christian Classics, 1968.

———. *On Consulting the Faithful in Matters of Doctrine.* Ed. John Coulson. London: Collins, 1986.

O'Collins, Gerald. *Retrieving Fundamental Theology.* New York: Paulist Press, 1993.

———. *Christology: A Biblical, Historical, and Systematic Study of Jesus.* New York: Oxford University Press, 1995.

Osborne, Kenan B. *Reconciliation and Justification.* New York: Paulist Press, 1990.

Phan, Peter C. *Grace and the Human Condition.* Wilmington, Del.: Michael Glazier, 1988.

Pontifical Biblical Commission. "The Historical Truth of the Gospels." In Joseph A. Fitzmyer, *A Christological Catechism.* Rev. and expanded ed. New York: Paulist Press, 1991, 119–64.

Power, David N. *The Eucharistic Mystery.* New York: Crossroad, 1993.

Rahner, Karl. *Foundations of Christian Faith.* Trans. William V. Dych. New York: Seabury Press, 1978.

Smolarski, Dennis C. *Sacred Mysteries: Sacramental Principles and Liturgical Practice.* New York: Paulist Press, 1995.

Sullivan, Francis A. *The Church We Believe In.* New York: Paulist Press, 1988.

———. *Salvation outside the Church?* New York: Paulist Press, 1992.

For readers interested in the writings of the Church Fathers, the following works in English are readily available:

Ancient Christian Writers. Currently 56 vols. New York: Paulist Press, 1946ff.

The Fathers of the Church. Currently 96 vols. Washington, D.C.: Catholic University of America Press, 1947ff.

Halton, Thomas, general editor. *Message of the Fathers of the Church.* Currently 22 vols. Collegeville, Minn.: Liturgical Press, 1983ff.

Jurgens, William A. *The Faith of the Early Fathers.* 3 vols. Collegeville, Minn.: Liturgical Press, 1970.

Ramsey, Boniface. *Beginning to Read the Fathers.* New York: Paulist Press, 1985.

Edward Wm. Clark is currently President/Rector of Saint John's Seminary College and Associate Professor of Theology at Saint John's Major Seminary, both located in Camarillo, California. Ordained a priest of the archdiocese of Los Angeles in 1972, Father Clark received his doctorate in theology from the Gregorian University in Rome in 1988. Since ordination, he has taught at all levels of Catholic education, from elementary school through university graduate courses, coordinated adult education programs, assisted in parochial ministry, and served as the Director of Religious Education and Formation for the fifty-two Catholic high schools of the archdiocese of Los Angeles.

OF RELATED INTEREST

William O'Malley, S.J.
WHY BE CATHOLIC?

"A dazzlingly original summary of the meaning of the
Catholic heritage, remarkably free of theological gibberish."
— ANDREW W. GREELEY

0-8245-1362-2; $11.95

William O'Malley, Mitch and Kathy Finley,
Kathleen Hughes, Barbara Quinn,
and Timothy E. O'Connell
THE PEOPLE'S CATECHISM
Catholic Faith for Adults

"*The People's Catechism* is true to its title!
It presents Catholicism as the living faith of a people.
Imagine, a catechism that is a delight? Here it is!"
— THOMAS H. GROOME

0-8245-1466-1; $ 14.95

Please support your local bookstore, or call 1-800-395-0690.
For a free catalog, please write us at
THE CROSSROAD PUBLISHING COMPANY
370 LEXINGTON AVENUE, NEW YORK, NY 10017

We hope you enjoyed Five Great Catholic Ideas. *Thank you for reading it.*

crossroad